グローバル社会で活躍する
ニッポン人を目指して

Gateway to the World of Global Business

英語で分かる
はじめての財務諸表
40日間トレーニング

経済たまごシリーズ**2**
【会計】

アルク
www.alc.co.jp

～はじめに～

　私たちの社会に浸透している「ビジネス界のグローバル化」。今や日常生活で使う身の回りの品から、国や企業が大型プロジェクトで扱う物資まであらゆる物が、世界中の国々が連携することによって流通し、私たちの生活を支えています。

　物ばかりではありません。情報も、言語という器に乗せて世界中を駆け巡っています。コンピューターを介したことでネットワークが飛躍的に広がる中、ビジネス界で用いられる共通言語として、英語がより重要になっていることは間違いありません。

　では、英語を使いこなすことができれば、グローバル化が進むビジネス社会で十分に通用する人材と言えるでしょうか。

　ビジネスの世界でワンランク上の人材に成長するためには、企業の経営的かつ財務的な体力を知るためのスキル——つまり、企業の財務諸表を解読する力が必要です。その力があれば、しかもそれを英語で行うことができれば、グローバル化の進むビジネスの世界で能力を存分に発揮できる人材となるはずです。

　この1冊を手元に置き、手になじむほどに活用していただくと、世界で活躍する企業の体力や動向が、数字から判断できるようになります。その結果、読者の皆さんのビジネス戦略・戦術の幅も広がっていくでしょう。数字を英語で理解する者は、ビジネス界を制する力を持つ——グローバル・ビジネスに躍り出るための入口は、本著の中にあります。本著を学ぶことでその扉を開き、ぜひとも前進していただきたいと思います。

編集部

CONTENTS

はじめに ……………………………………………………………………………… 3
本書の使い方 ………………………………………………………………………… 6
CDの構成と使い方 …………………………………………………………………… 7

Chapter 1　財務諸表は「会社の体力」を映す鏡　—貸借対照表—

1日目	短期的な安定性を財務諸表で確認……………………………………… 10
2日目	安定性を示す、もうひとつの指標……………………………………… 14
3日目	なぜ、花王はカネボウの化粧品部門を買収したか？…………………… 18
4日目	トヨタが無借金経営でない理由………………………………………… 24
5日目	外資ファンドに狙われる企業、その貸借対照表……………………… 30
6日目	自己資本率の高い会社が狙われる理由………………………………… 34
7日目	なぜ、イオンはダイエーを子会社にしないのか？…………………… 38
8日目	REVIEW EXERCISE…………………………………………………… 42

Chapter 2　国家財政が破綻しない不思議　—損益計算書—

9日目	損益計算書とは？………………………………………………………… 48
10日目	売上原価と製造原価の違い……………………………………………… 54
11日目	利益の種類と、販売費および一般管理費……………………………… 58
12日目	当期純利益の算出方法とさまざまな損益……………………………… 62
13日目	日本の財政赤字とプライマリーバランス……………………………… 66
14日目	国の財政問題で問われるスピード……………………………………… 70
15日目	日本政府が破綻しない理由……………………………………………… 74
16日目	REVIEW EXERCISE…………………………………………………… 78

Chapter 3　リニアモーターカーが進まない事情　—キャッシュフロー—

17日目	キャッシュフロー計算書と営業キャッシュフロー …………………… 84
18日目	お金が出て行かない費用とは？………………………………………… 88
19日目	投資キャッシュフローと未来投資……………………………………… 92
20日目	日産のV字回復と未来投資……………………………………………… 96

経済たまごシリーズ② 【会計】
英語で分かる　はじめての財務諸表 40日間トレーニング
Let's study how to read financial statements in English

21日目	キャッシュフロー経営の基本は「稼ぐ」と「使う」	100
22日目	ＤＣＦと会社の価値の上げ方	104
23日目	政府のキャッシュフロー計算書	108
24日目	最優先されるべきは「人材育成」	112
25日目	REVIEW EXERCISE	116

Chapter 4　ブランドが大好き、IT企業　—損益分岐点—

26日目	新しい収益構造を持つ企業の誕生	122
27日目	固定費と変動費——変動費率を低く抑えろ！	126
28日目	ＩＴ産業の特徴は「良いとこ取り」	130
29日目	固定費も変動費も少なくて済む事業を求めて	134
30日目	なぜ、航空券には格安チケットがあるのか？	138
31日目	割引販売のない新幹線	142
32日目	「増し分」利益を得ている業界は？	146
33日目	REVIEW EXERCISE	150

Chapter 5　液晶テレビ、みるみる値下がり　—直接原価計算—

34日目	設備投資と製品価格	156
35日目	減価償却のマジック	160
36日目	ダンピングと、日本の固定費処理	164
37日目	財務・管理・税務の３つの会計	168
38日目	直接原価計算をしてみよう！	172
39日目	２種類の原価計算方法と利益の意味	176
40日目	REVIEW EXERCISE	180

COLUMN 　46／82／120／154

INDEX（英語／日本語）　184／187

本書の構成

本書は、財務や会計のテーマ別に5つのChapterに分かれており、1日1スキットずつ学習できるよう構成されています。各Chapterの終わりには、チャンツを含むReview Exerciseが設けられているので、問題に挑戦して、学習した内容を整理してください。

① CDに収録されている、教授と学生の会話のスクリプトです。

最初はスクリプトを見ないで、音声だけを繰り返し聞きましょう。CDの音声に重ねて発音する練習を行うと、聞く力だけでなく、話す力も伸ばすことができます。

②財務諸表や会計の基礎を理解するための重要語です。

重要な語句を、日英で対応させて覚えましょう。英文スクリプトと日本語訳中の該当語句に色が付いていますので、英語の発音と、使われている文脈を確認してください。

③ CDに収録されている会話の日本語訳です。

会話を聞いて大体の意味が分かった後で、確認や理解を深めるために読みましょう。英語の会話を繰り返し聞いても意味があまり分からないときは、ここを読んで大意をつかんでから再度、英語を聞きましょう。

④覚えておきたい単語や、英語特有の言い回しです。

その日のスキットで使われていた語句から、覚えておきたい言い回しや単語を抜粋しました。英文を聞く前に、これらの語句にだけ目を通しておくのもおススメです。

⑤チャンツと練習問題からなるReview Exerciseです。

そのChapterに登場したKeywordsとWords & Phrasesから重要語句を選び出し、チャンツに乗せて収録しました。CDに合わせて発音を練習してください。続いて、右ページの問題を解いて、そのChapterで学習したことを確認し、理解を定着させましょう。

CDの構成と使い方

　本テキストのCDには、5つのChapterからなる合計35のスキットと、Chapterごとの復習用のチャンツが収録されています。各ページでは、🅘TR02 の数字が、CDとトラックの番号を表しています。

　CDとトラック番号とSkitの対応表は以下の通りです。学習したいトラックを呼び出して、繰り返し聞いたり、後について言ったりするのにお使いください。

▼トラック一覧表
＊ Track 1 には本の英語タイトルが収録されています

CD番号	Track番号		Skit内容
CD1	2	Chapter 1	1日目
	3		2日目
	4		3日目
	5		4日目
	6		5日目
	7		6日目
	8		7日目
	9		8日目 チャンツ
	10	Chapter 2	9日目
	11		10日目
	12		11日目
	13		12日目
	14		13日目
	15		14日目
	16		15日目
	17		16日目 チャンツ
	18	Chapter 3	17日目
	19		18日目
	20		19日目
	21		20日目
	22		21日目
	23		22日目
	24		23日目
	25		24日目
	26		25日目 チャンツ

CD番号	Track番号		Skit内容
CD2	2	Chapter 4	26日目
	3		27日目
	4		28日目
	5		29日目
	6		30日目
	7		31日目
	8		32日目
	9		33日目 チャンツ
	10	Chapter 5	34日目
	11		35日目
	12		36日目
	13		37日目
	14		38日目
	15		39日目
	16		40日目 チャンツ

～登場人物の紹介～

本書は、小浜教授と、大学3年生で小浜ゼミに所属するマキの会話で学習が進行していきます。

Prof. Obama:
経営分析と管理会計が専門の大学教授。学生の面倒見がよい

Maki:
将来海外で働くことを夢見て、英語で財務諸表を勉強している

【CD ご使用上の注意】
- 弊社制作の音声 CD は、CD プレーヤーでの再生を保証する規格品です。
- パソコンでご使用になる場合、CD-ROM ドライブとの相性により、ディスクを再生できない場合がございます。ご了承ください。
- パソコンでタイトル・トラック情報を表示させたい場合は、iTunes をご利用ください。iTunes では、弊社が CD のタイトル・トラック情報を登録している Gracenote 社の CDDB（データベース）からインターネットを介してトラック情報を取得することができます。
- CD として正常に音声が再生できるディスクからパソコンや mp3 プレーヤー等への取り込み時にトラブルが生じた際は、まず、そのアプリケーション（ソフト）やプレーヤーの製作元・製造元へご相談ください。

Chapter 1

財務諸表は「会社の体力」を映す鏡

ココを見て判断！ —貸借対照表—

Chapter 1

Maki: Have you heard of the book, "How to Read Financial Statements in a Second"? I saw it in a bookstore.

Prof. Obama: Yes, I've read it. It was more interesting than I expected.

Maki: Really? But, surely it's impossible to read a financial statement in a second, isn't it?

Obama: Sure, it is. But, if you only have one second, where do you look specifically in the financial statements of a company?

Maki: At the net earnings?

Obama: The net earnings are important, but companies go bankrupt even when they make a profit.

Maki: Well, the most important thing must be whether the company is going to go bankrupt or not.

Obama: It probably is. Whether you're going to do business with the company, or going to work for them, it's more important that the company can continue to exist rather than whether it's making a profit or not.

Maki: Well, how about a large amount of loans?

Obama: Loans are called liabilities in financial statements. Even if the liabilities are big, the company doesn't go bankrupt if it has bigger assets to cover the liabilities. This is the important point to check. So, the answer is to compare the top figure in the left and the right columns of the balance sheet.

Maki: Do you mean the current assets and the current liabilities?

Obama: Yes. The figure you get when you divide current assets by current liabilities is called the current ratio, and that's what

Keywords

負債
liabilities
銀行からの融資や社債で調達された、特定の期限までに返済しなければならないか、商品やサービスなどを提供しなければならないお金。他人資本、借金。

貸借対照表
balance sheet
バランスシート。資金がどこから調達され、どのような資産の取得に使われたかを示す。左半分の「資産」の部と、右半分の「負債」および「純資産」の部の2つに分かれる。

流動資産
current assets
現預金や売掛金、棚卸資産（在庫）など、すぐ資金化できるか、すぐに使う資産。

流動負債
current liabilities
通常1年以内に返済する義務のある負債。

流動比率
current ratio
流動負債の返済能力を見る指標の1つ。
〔流動比率＝流動資産÷流動負債〕

Translation

マキ：『「1秒！」で財務諸表を読む方法』って本のこと、聞いたことありますか？　私、本屋で見かけたんですけど。

小浜教授：ああ、もう読んだよ。意外とこの本、面白かったな。

マキ：ホントですか？　でも、1秒で財務諸表を読むなんて、とても無理なんじゃないですか？

小浜：もちろんそうさ。でも、1秒しかないときに財務諸表の特にどこを見るかって聞かれたら、どこかな？

マキ：当期利益かなあ？

小浜：当期利益も大事だけど、黒字が出ているのに倒産する会社もあるからね。

マキ：先生、倒産するかどうかが一番大事なんですか？

小浜：そうだろうね。その会社と取引をするにしても、その会社に就職するにしても、まずは、そこが儲かっているかどうかより、存続できるかどうかの方が大事だからね。

マキ：じゃ、借金が多いとかは？

小浜：借金——これは、財務諸表では負債と呼ぶんだけど——仮にこの負債が多くても、それを払えるだけの大きな資産があれば会社はつぶれないだろう？　そこを見るのが大事なんだ。つまり正解は、財務諸表の中でも、貸借対照表の左と右のトップに書いてある数字を比べることさ。

マキ：この「流動資産」と「流動負債」を、ですか？

小浜：そうだ。流動資産を流動負債で割った数字を流動比率と言うんだが、この

you should check when you look at financial statements in a second.

Maki: What kind of figure is acceptable? Is it more than 100%, as the company should have more assets than liabilities?

Obama: It depends on the company, but it's usually above the range of 60% to 120%.

Maki: Really? That's lower than I thought.

Obama: If it's above that range, there's little risk of going bankrupt. To check the stability of the company, you need to see the short-term liquidity, if you have another second. Short-term liquidity is the figure you get when you divide cash in banks plus immediately salable securities by the monthly sales, that is, one-twelfth of the company's annual sales.

Maki: What kind of figure is acceptable for short-term liquidity?

Obama: It depends on the company's size and the industry. As an approximate guideline, it's one month for a large company and 1.5 months for a medium or small company.

current ratio = current assets ÷ current liabilities

current assets	○○○	current liabilities	○○○
		fixed liabilities	○○○
fixed assets	○○○	net assets	○○○

$$\text{short-term liquidity} = \frac{\text{cash} + \text{immediately saleable assets}}{\text{monthly sales}}$$

KEYWORDS

手元流動性
short-term liquidity

企業経営上、短期的に最も重要となる指標で、企業の安定性を示す。現預金と、年間売上高を12分の1にした月商との比率。

〔(現預金＋すぐに売れる有価証券等)÷月商〕

この関係(流動比率＝流動資産÷流動負債)を見る！

流動資産 ○○○	流動負債 ○○○
	固定負債 ○○○
固定資産 ○○○	純資産 ○○○

大切！　手元流動性 ＝ (現預金＋すぐに資金化できるもの) ／ 月商

比率こそが、1秒で財務諸表を見るときにチェックすべきポイントさ。

マキ：流動比率はどれくらいあればいいんですか？　負債を賄えるだけの資産がなくちゃいけないから、100％以上ですか？

小浜：企業によっても違うけれど、60％～120％以上だな。

マキ：へえー、意外に少なくていいんですね。

小浜：その幅以上なら倒産するリスクはほとんどないってことだね。ただ、もう1秒あるなら、会社の安定性を見るという観点からは手元流動性を見なくちゃいけない。手元流動性とは、その会社の預金とすぐに売れる有価証券などを足した額を、月商、すなわち、その会社の年間の売上高を12分の1にしたもので割った数字だ。

マキ：手元流動性はどれくらいあれば、安心ですか？

小浜：それは、会社の規模や業種によっても違うけれど、目安としては、大企業なら1カ月分、中小企業なら1.5カ月分くらいないと心配だな。

Words & Phrases
①②③……は、その語が登場した行数を表しています。

- ⑧ specifically　特に、具体的に
- ⑩ go bankrupt　破産する
- ⑰ make a profit　儲ける、利益を生む
- ㉑ cover　〜の費用として足りる
- ㉒ figure　数量、価格
- ㉓ column　列
- ㉙ acceptable　条件を満たしている
- ㉟ stability　安定性、持続性
- ㊳ immediately　すぐさま、即座に
- ㊳ salable　売れる、売却できる
- ㊳ securities　有価証券、債券
- ㊴ one-twelfth　(分数で)12分の1
- ㊴ annual　1年の、年次の
- ㊶ industry　産業、(業種としての)業
- ㊷ approximate　おおよその、概略の
- ㊷ guideline　指針

Chapter 1

2日目 安定性を示す、もうひとつの指標

Maki: What are the other financial statements besides balance sheets?

Prof. Obama: The principal financial statements are the balance sheet, income statement, or profit and loss statement, and cash flow statement. These are called the three financial statements. For the moment, just remember these three.

Maki: Are there any other figures on these financial statements, besides current ratio and short-term liquidity that indicate the stability of a company?

Obama: Yes, there are. First, look at the balance sheets.

Maki: Well, the left side shows how the money has been used—I mean, how the money has been used for operations. And the right side shows how the money has been collected. Or to put it another way, it shows how the money has been financed.

Obama: Now, let's have a closer look at the financing. There are two methods of financing. One is liabilities, and the other is net assets, or capital. These items are very important when you learn about financial statements. Do you know the difference between them?

Maki: No, I don't. How are they different?

Obama: Roughly speaking, a liability is the money that must be returned sooner or later, while a net asset is the money that doesn't need to be returned unless the company is liquidated.

Maki: So, it's better to get money for operations by increasing net assets as much as possible without increasing liability, if possible.

Keywords

損益計算書
income statement / profit and loss statement

一定期間の企業の損益状況を表したもの。財務諸表の1つ。income statement が米式で、profit and loss statement が英式の呼び方。

キャッシュフロー計算書
cash flow statement

企業活動に当てる現金や預金の流れを示すもの。日本では2000年3月期から財務諸表に組み込まれ、営業・投資・財務の3種類の内訳からなる。

財務諸表
financial statements

貸借対照表、損益計算書などからなる、企業の経営状況を判断するための指標。
貸借対照表＋損益計算書＋キャッシュフロー計算書＝「財務三表」

純資産（または資本）
net assets / capital

返済しなくてよい資金。資本金や、利益の蓄積である利益剰余金を指す。

Translation

マキ：ところで先生、財務諸表って、貸借対照表のほかに何があるんですか？

小浜教授：貸借対照表と、損益計算書、キャッシュフロー計算書が代表的な財務諸表で、この3つを「財務三表」と呼ぶんだ。当面、この3表だけ覚えておけばよろしい。

マキ：その財務諸表上で会社の安定性を見るために必要な数字は、流動比率と手元流動性のほかにもあるんですか？

小浜：あるとも。まずは貸借対照表を見てごらん。

マキ：えーと、左側はお金の使い道、つまり、どのように資金が運用されたかが示されています。そして右側は、どうやってお金を集めたか、つまり、カッコよく言うと、資金がどうやって調達されたかが描かれているんですね。

小浜：じゃあ、その「資金調達」ってものに注目してみよう。資金を調達するには、負債と純資産（または資本）という2通りの方法がある。実はこれが、財務諸表を学ぶ上でとても重要な項目なんだ。さあ、何が違うんだろう？

マキ：えー、分かりません。どう違うんですか？

小浜：大ざっぱに言えば、負債はいずれ返済しなければいけないお金。一方の純資産は、会社を解散でもしない限り、返済する必要のないお金さ。

マキ：じゃあ、なるべくなら、負債を多くしないで、純資産をできるだけ増やして資金を運用すればいいってことですか？

Obama: Yes. Now, the figure that you get when you divide net assets by total assets is called the equity ratio. It's a very important figure, as it shows the ratio of money that doesn't have to be returned.

Maki: Is there a guideline figure for equity ratio?

Obama: It depends on the industry. In the manufacturing industry where a great amount of fixed assets are required, the minimum will be 20%, and in the trading industry where a great amount of current assets are required, the minimum will be 15%. In any industry, if the equity ratio is less than 10%, it is unstable, and the company is described as undercapitalized.

Maki: I thought a company was more stable the nearer the equity ratio was to 100%.

Obama: Well, things are not so simple. Management and the economy are not static, but always moving and dynamic.

Maki: But, I can't get a clear picture of what that means.

Obama: All right. I'll explain using an actual case.

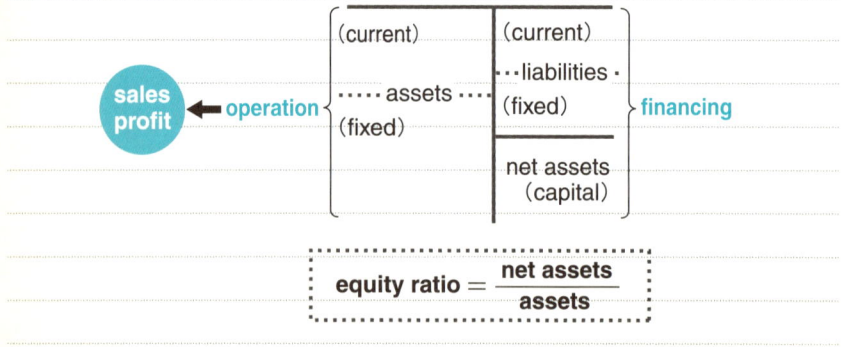

KEYWORDS

自己資本比率
equity ratio

資産を賄っている（企業経営に使っている）資金のうち、返済する必要のない資金の比率を表す。
〔自己資本比率＝純資産÷資産〕

固定資産
fixed assets

企業が継続的に自ら使用する目的で有する資産。土地・建物や備品などの「有形固定資産」、営業権や商標権、特許権などの「無形固定資産」、長期保有株式などの「投資目的資産」からなる。

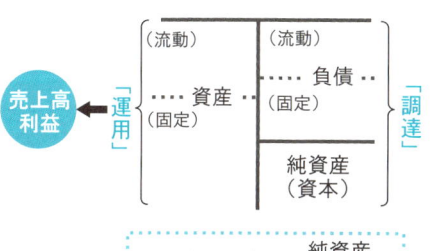

小浜：その通り。純資産を資産で割った数字を自己資本比率というんだが、これは、会社経営に使う資金のうち、返済する必要のない資金の比率を表す、とても大事な数字だね。

マキ：自己資本比率の目安は、どのくらいですか？

小浜：業種によって違うが、製造業のように固定資産を多く必要とする会社なら20％、商社のように流動資産を多く要する会社なら15％くらいが最低限度かな。ただ、どんな業種であれ、自己資本比率が10％以下だと、安定性に欠けていて、その会社は過小資本と見なされる。

マキ：あれ？　自己資本比率が100％に近ければ近いほど、会社が安定するんだと思ってました。

小浜：う〜ん、実はそう単純にはいかないんだ。経済とか経営というのは、じっとそこにある静的なものじゃなくて、常に動いている動的なものだからね。

マキ：でも、具体的なイメージが浮かばないですよ。

小浜：じゃあ、現実にあるケースを使って説明しよう。

Words & Phrases   ①②③……は、その語が登場した行数を表しています。

① besides　〜のほかに、に加えて
③ principal　主たる、重要な
⑥ for the moment　差し当たり、当分の間は
⑧ indicate　指し示す、示唆する
⑫ operation　事業、運営、経営
⑬ collect　集める
⑬ to put it another way　別の言い方をすれば
⑮ financing　資金調達
㉑ roughly　大雑把に、概略で
㉓ liquidate　（会社を）解体する、（負債を）清算する
㉜ manufacturing　製造（業）の
㉝ amount　量、額
㊲ describe 〜 as　〜を……と描写する
㊲ undercapitalized　資金不足の

Chapter 1

なぜ、花王はカネボウの
化粧品部門を買収したか？

Prof. Obama: These are the consolidated balance sheets of Kao Corporation for the fiscal years 2005 and 2006.* What do you find by comparing the two years?

Maki: I find that the total assets were doubled, and the total liabilities were tripled.

Obama: Yes, that's right. In these periods, Kao purchased the cosmetics division of Kanebo. What is important is that the money needed for the purchase was procured by bank loans. Therefore, the liabilities have increased. The important point of this purchase is that the money was procured not by issuing shares but, as I said, by bank loans. If we calculate the equity ratio, it's 65.1% for fiscal year 2005 and 41.8% for fiscal year 2006.

Maki: That's a tremendous decrease. Isn't that a serious problem?

Obama: As a matter of fact, they intentionally increased the liabilities with interest and lowered the equity ratio for financial and strategic purposes. Kao purchased Kanebo to strengthen Kao's cosmetics division as a sales strategy. By obtaining the Kanebo brand they can aim for a bigger market share and more effective global marketing.

Maki: Intentionally? Were Kao trying to show that their company was in trouble to avoid the possibility of being purchased?

Obama: That's not the main reason. In fact, the real reason is more mundane. They wanted to lower the procurement cost of the purchase of Kanebo. What kinds of ways to procure money are there?

Maki: Liabilities and net assets, or capital.

KEYWORDS

連結貸借対照表
consolidated balance sheets

実質的に支配従属関係にある複数の企業からなるグループ（親会社・子会社・関連会社）を1つの企業と見立てて、その経営成績・財務状況を示す、連結財務諸表の1つ。

有利子負債
liabilities with interest

金融機関からの借入金や社債、債券市場からの社債や転換社債、コマーシャル・ペーパーなど、企業が利子をつけて返済しなければならない負債。

TRANSLATION

小浜教授：これは、2005年と2006年の花王の連結貸借対照表*だ。で、この2つの表を比べて、どうかな？

マキ：あっ、資産が2倍、それに、負債が3倍に増えていますね。

小浜：そうなんだ。この期間中に、花王はカネボウの化粧品部門を買収したんだ。ここで重要なのは、その買収資金を花王が銀行融資（＝負債）で調達したということなんだ。だから負債が増えているんだ。繰り返すけど、増資するのでなく、借入金で賄ったところに、この買収のポイントがある。自己資本比率を計算してみると、2005年が65.1％で、2006年が41.8％。

マキ：激減ですね！　これってマジでまずいんじゃないですか？

小浜：実は花王は、財務戦略上、わざと有利子負債を増やして、自己資本比率を下げたんだ。花王がカネボウを買収したのは、営業戦略上、化粧品部門を強化するためだ。カネボウのブランドを手に入れて、シェアアップと、グローバル展開における収益力のアップを狙ったからでもある。

マキ：わざとですか？　もしかして、買収されないようにしようとして、わざと危なく見せようとしたとか？

小浜：それが主な理由じゃない。実はその理由はもっと現実的で、カネボウを買収する資金の調達コストを下げるためだったんだ。資金の調達方法には何と何があったっけ？

マキ：負債と純資産（資本）でしたよね。

＊花王の連結貸借対照表（2005年、2006年）は、22－23ページを参照。

● Chapter 1　3日目

Obama: You're right. In Japan, it has become possible to get bank loans at an extremely low interest rate since the end of the bubble economy. On the other hand, net assets, or capital, is originally the money that a company receives from its shareholders. Shareholders invest their money in a company because they think the return from investment will be higher than that from government bonds.

　This extra amount above the government bond interest level is called a risk premium, and can now be expected to be at least 5%, even in an excellent company. In short, if you receive bank loans in the market, the interest is at most 1-2%, while government bond interest plus risk premium often exceeds 7%. So, in order to lower the procurement cost of money, bank loans were used to cover the purchase money. As a result, the equity ratio was drastically reduced.

Maki: In other words, the procurement cost of liabilities is lower than the procurement cost of net assets. So, it isn't good for the equity ratio to be too high, is it?

Obama: That's right. There is another ratio to be used when we consider the procurement cost of money. It's the weighted average of cost of capital, or WACC for short.

the financing cost of liabilities and capital

assets
- liabilities
  - liabilities without interest → zero cost
  - liabilities with interest → interest (rate)
- net assets
  - shareholder's expected return = the government bond interest + α

KEYWORDS

リスクプレミアム
risk premium

金融商品に関して、リスクに対して支払われる対価。例えば国債はリスクがほとんどないのに対して、リスクがある分、株式の期待収益率は高くなり、この利回りの差がリスクプレミアムとなる。

加重平均資本調達コスト（WACC）
weighted average of cost of capital
☞ 4日目

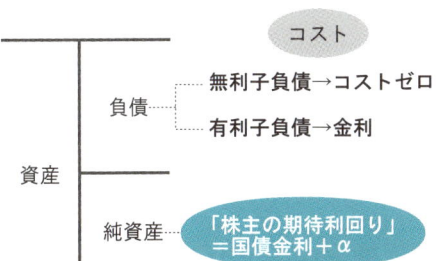

負債と資本の調達コスト

小浜：その通り。日本ではバブルが弾けてから、融資が超低金利で受けられるようになっている。一方、純資産（資本）の方は、もとはと言えば株主から預かっているお金だ。株主が会社に投資するのは、会社に託した方が国債を買うよりも利回りが良いと判断するからだ。
　この国債金利を上回るプラスαをリスクプレミアムというのだが、優良会社でもこれが最低5％は期待されているんだ。要するに、市場で融資を受けると、金利はせいぜい1〜2％。一方、国債＋リスクプレミアムだと7％を超えるのはざら。そこで、資金の調達コストを下げるためにわざと、負債で買収資金を賄ったんだ。その結果、自己資本比率が大きく減少したってわけさ。

マキ：つまり、負債の調達コストの方が、純資産の調達コストよりも安い。だから、自己資本比率が高すぎるのもよくない、ってことですね。

小浜：そうなんだ。それともうひとつ、資金調達コストを考えるのに用いる比率があるんだけど、それは、負債の調達コストと純資産の調達コストを加重平均したもので、加重平均資本調達コスト、略してWACCと言うんだ。

Words & Phrases
①②③……は、その語が登場した行数を表しています。

- ② fiscal year　営業年度、事業年度
- ⑥ purchase　購入する、獲得する
- ⑦ division　部門、事業部。cosmetics division で「化粧品部門」
- ⑩ issue　発行する。issuing shares で「株式の発行」
- ⑪ calculate　計算する、算出する
- ⑬ tremendous　おびただしい、途方もない
- ⑬ decrease　減少
- ⑭ intentionally　わざと、意図的に
- ⑯ strategic　戦略上の
- ⑰ obtain　手に入れる、取得する
- ㉓ mundane　俗世の、ありふれた
- ㉘ extremely　極めて、非常に
- ㉚ shareholder　株主
- ㉛ invest　投資する
- ㉜ return　リターン、利回り
- ㉜ investment　投資
- ㊳ exceed　超える、上回る
- ㊶ drastically　大幅に、抜本的に
- ㊼ for short　略して言うと

Kao Corporation
Consolidated Balance Sheets

(Million of yen)

	FY2005 March 31, 2006	Composition %	FY2004 March 31, 2005	Composition %
Assets				
Current assets	364,613	29.9	289,180	42.0
Fixed assets	855,872	70.1	399,662	58.0
Tangible assets	282,796	23.1	260,223	37.8
Intangible assets	466,221	38.2	86,222	12.5
Investments and other assets	106,854	8.8	53,217	7.7
Deferred assets	77	0.0	130	0.0
Total assets	1,220,564	100.0	688,973	100.0
Liabilities				
Current liabilities	436,193	35.7	211,541	30.7
Notes and accounts payable - trade	96,507		70,993	
Short-term debt	166,759		18,604	
Current portion of convertible bonds	—		2,596	
Current portion of long-term debt	22,699		91	
⋮	⋮	⋮	⋮	⋮
Long-term liabilities	265,790	21.8	21,768	3.1
Long-term debt	218,545		1,426	
⋮	⋮	⋮	⋮	⋮
Total liabilities	701,983	57.5	233,310	33.8
Minority interests	8,903	0.7	7,413	1.1
Shareholders' equity	509,676	41.8	448,249	65.1
Total liabilities, minority interests	1,220,564	100.0	688,973	100.0

花王の連結貸借対照表

(単位:百万円)

科目	期別	平成17年3月31日現在 金額	構成比%	平成18年3月31日現在 金額	構成比%
(資産の部)					
Ⅰ 流動資産		289,180	42.0	364,613	29.9
Ⅱ 固定資産		399,662	58.0	855,872	70.1
1. 有形固定資産		260,223	37.8	282,796	23.1
2. 無形固定資産		86,222	12.5	466,221	38.2
3. 投資その他の資産		53,217	7.7	106,854	8.8
Ⅲ 繰延資産		130	0.0	77	0.0
資産合計		688,973	100.0	1,220,564	100.0
(負債の部)					
Ⅰ 流動負債		211,541	30.7	436,193	35.7
支払手形及び買掛金		70,993		96,507	
短期借入金		18,604		166,759	
一年以内に償還予定の転換社債		2,596		—	
一年以内に返済予定の長期借入金		91		22,699	
︙		︙	︙	︙	︙
Ⅱ 固定負債		21,768	3.1	265,790	21.8
長期借入金		1,426		218,545	
︙		︙	︙	︙	︙
負債合計		233,310	33.8	701,983	57.5
(少数株主持分)					
少数株主持分		7,413	1.1	8,903	0.7
資本合計		448,249	65.1	509,676	41.8
負債、少数株主持分及び資本合計		688,973	100.0	1,220,564	100.0

3倍

8割増加

Chapter 1

4日目 トヨタが無借金経営でない理由

Maki: Prof. Obama, WACC is an index to measure the procurement cost of money, isn't it? To have a weighted average of two kinds of procurement costs of money means that the higher the percentage of the procurement cost of net assets, the higher the WACC. Is that right?

Prof. Obama: Yes, it is. The higher the WACC is, the higher the procurement cost of money is. Therefore, the expected profit to be gained by using the net assets will be higher. There is another index called ROA, which is the profit rate you see by using total assets. It is the figure you get when you divide operating profit by total assets. In conclusion, ROA must be higher than WACC, because WACC is cost, and ROA is profit. ROA is a very important index. You need to remember it very well.

Maki: Now, I know that ROA is obtained by dividing operating profit by assets, but how is it related to lowering the equity ratio?

Obama: Good question! If the equity ratio is high, the WACC is high. The shareholders will not be satisfied unless the ROA is high enough to exceed the high WACC. As a result, the stock price will become lower. So, the aim is to lower the hurdle of the ROA by increasing liabilities and by lowering the WACC. Kao used this mechanism to purchase Kanebo.

Maki: Now, I am gradually getting used to the logic. At first, financial statements seemed to be quite difficult to understand. But once you start to understand, they're quite interesting.

Obama: Yes, they're like medical examination reports. By looking closely at the figures, getting the ratios and comparing the

KEYWORDS

WACC（加重平均資本調達コスト）
weighted average of cost of capital
負債と純資産を加重平均して算出する、資本の調達コスト。自己資本率が高い（純資産が大きい）企業の方が数値は高くなる。
☞3日目

純資産
net assets
☞2日目

ROA（資産利益率）
return on assets
企業の収益率を示す代表的な指標の1つで、資産の効率性を示す。一定の資産をどの程度有効に活用し、その結果としての利益を得ているかを測るもの。

〔ROA ＝営業利益÷資産〕

$$ROA \geqq WACC$$
　　↑　　　　↑
　利益　　調達コスト

負債
liabilities
☞1日目

TRANSLATION

マキ：小浜先生。WACCというのは、資金調達のコストを測る指標なんですよね。（負債と純資産という）2種類の調達コストを加重平均するってことは、純資産の調達コストの割合が多くなればなるほど、WACCも高くなるってことで合ってますか？

小浜教授：そう、その通りだ。WACCが高くなるということは、すなわち、資金の調達コストが高くなること。だから、資産を使って得られるべき利益の期待値も高くなる。資産を使った利益率を表すROA（資産利益率）という指標があるんだけど、これは、営業利益を資産で割った数字だ。結論から言えば、ROAはWACCより高くなければならないんだ。なぜなら、WACCはコストで、ROAは利益だからね。ROAはとても大事な指標だから、しっかり覚えてね。

マキ：はい、「ROA＝営業利益÷資産」ですね。でもそれと自己資本比率を下げることと、どう関係があるのですか？

小浜：いい質問だ！　自己資本比率が高いとWACCが高くなり、それに応じて高いWACCを上回る高いROAを稼ぎ出さないと株主が満足しない。すると（株式市場での評価が下がって）結果的に株価が下がりかねないからね。だから、負債を増やしてWACCを下げることによって、ROAのハードルを下げることが狙いなんだ。花王のカネボウ買収にはこんなカラクリがあったんだね。

マキ：なんだか、ちょっと分かってきたような気がする。財務諸表って最初は難しくて、とっつきにくかったけど、分かってくると面白いかも。

小浜：そう。財務諸表というのは、健康診断書のようなところがあるんだ。書いてある数字をじっくり見て、比率を

current year with the previous one, you can see what condition a company is in, and some of the strategies it is using. For example, let's look at the consolidated balance sheets of Toyota Motor Corporation.*

Maki: I'm surprised. Toyota is a globally active company, but it has as much as 12 trillion yen in liabilities with interest.

Obama: It is surprising, isn't it? People say that Toyota is a debt-free company. If you look at their balance sheets, they have 12 trillion yen in liabilities with interest against total assets of 32.6 trillion yen. Toyota is globally expanding their business and they surely need a vast amount of money. On the other hand, their net income is 1.6 trillion yen. If they don't do anything, their income will keep on increasing their net assets (capital). As the procurement cost of net assets is much higher than that of liabilities, Toyota intentionally procured liabilities with interest, thus lowering the WACC by expanding both total assets and total liabilities on their balance sheets. That's my opinion anyway.

Maki: Wow, it's amazing that we can even see their intentions.

KEYWORDS

有利子負債
liabilities with interest
☞ 3日目

純利益
net income
企業が最終的に得る利益。経常利益から株主配当、特別損益、法人税などの税金を差し引いた後に残った利益で、その会計年度における企業の経営成績を示す。当期利益、当期純利益、税引き後利益と呼ぶ場合もある。net income、net profit は英式。米式では、net earnings。

出したり、その年と前年とを比べてみたりすることで、その会社の状態や戦略の一部なんかも読み取ることができるんだ。例えば、2007年度のトヨタ自動車の連結貸借対照表＊を見てみよう。

マキ：驚いた。トヨタって世界的に活躍している企業なのに、有利子負債が12兆円もある。

小浜：驚きだろう？　トヨタは無借金経営と言われているからね。貸借対照表をよく見ると、32.6兆円の総資産に対し、なんと12兆円の有利子負債がある。もちろん、トヨタはグローバルに事業を拡大していて、それだけ資金需要も旺盛だ。その一方、トヨタは毎年1.6兆円もの純利益を出しているから、放っておくと利益がたまって純資産（資本）がどんどん増えてしまう。純資産の調達コストは負債のコストよりずっと高いから、トヨタはわざと有利子負債を調達して、貸借対照表の資産と負債の両面を膨らませることによって WACC を下げている、僕にはこう読めるんだ。

マキ：すごい、そんな狙いまで分かるんですね！

＊トヨタ自動車の連結貸借対照表（2007年度）は、28－29ページを参照。

Words & Phrases
①②③……は、その語が登場した行数を表しています。

- ① index　指標、指数
- ① measure　測定する
- ⑧ gain　（努力して）獲得する
- ⑪ in conclusion　結論として、要するに
- ⑮ related to　〜に関連している
- ⑮ lower　下げる
- ⑰ satisfied　満足した、納得した
- ⑱ stock price　株価
- ㉒ get used to　〜に慣れる、なじんでくる
- ㉕ examination　検査、調査。medical examination report で「健康診断書」
- ㉗ previous　以前の、前回の
- ㉛ globally　全世界的に
- ㉜ trillion　兆
- ㉝ -free　〜のない、〜が含まれていない
- ㊱ expand　拡大する
- ㊲ vast　膨大な、巨額の
- ㊺ amazing　驚くべき、素晴らしい

TOYOTA MOTOR CORPORATION
CONSOLIDATED BALANCE SHEETS

(All financial information has been prepared in accordance with accounting principles generally accepted in the United States of America)

(Amounts are rounded to the nearest million yen)

	FY2007 (As of March 31, 2007)
Liabilities	
Current liabilities:	11,767,170
Short-term borrowings	3,497,391
Current portion of long-term debt	2,368,116
⋮	⋮
Long-term liabilities:	8,343,273
Long-term debt	6,263,585
⋮	⋮
Total liabilities	20,110,443
Minority interest in consolidated subsidiaries	628,244
Shareholders' equity	
Common stock	397,050
⋮	⋮
Total shareholders' equity	11,836,092
Total liabilities and shareholders' equity	32,574,779

トヨタ自動車の連結貸借対照表

(平成19年3月期：百万円未満四捨五入)

科目	当期(19.3末現在)
(負債の部)	百万円
流動負債	11,767,170
<u>短期借入債務</u>	<u>3,497,391</u>
<u>1年以内に返済予定の長期借入債務</u>	<u>2,368,116</u>
：	：
固定負債	8,343,273
<u>長期借入債務</u>	<u>6,263,585</u>
：	：
負債合計	20,110,443
(少数株主持分)	
少数株主持分	628,244
(資本の部)	
資本金	397,050
：	：
資本合計	11,836,092
負債・少数株主持分及び資本合計	32,574,779

Chapter 1

外資ファンドに狙われる企業
その貸借対照表

Prof. Obama: Now, let's study an attempted buy-out, using an actual case. You probably know about the takeover bid for Bull-Dog Sauce made by an American fund, Steel Partners, as it was widely reported in the mass media. Why do you think Bull-Dog Sauce was targeted?

Maki: Well, to purchase a company is to become a shareholder of that company, isn't it? So, if you want to make money by becoming a shareholder, for example, you are likely to make a big profit by selling the company assets at a high price or by selling your stock to another company who wants to buy it.

Obama: Yes, that's right. You're thinking like the manager of a buy-out fund now. That's one very important way of thinking, but, here, let's think about how it relates to balance sheets. Companies with a high equity ratio and a low ROE are often targeted.

Maki: ROE? What's ROE?

Obama: ROE stands for return on equity, and it is the figure you get when you divide net income by net assets. Do you know the difference between ROA and ROE?

Maki: We use operating income for ROA, but net income for ROE. Why do we use different types of income?

Obama: I'm glad you noticed the difference, because it's very important. The reason we use net income for ROE is that ROE is used to calculate the profit ratio to the money received from shareholders. There are various kinds of profit, but the profit attributed to shareholders must be the net income after paying

KEYWORDS

買収
buy-out
ここでは「企業買収」を指す。経営効率や製品の付加価値を高めるために、既存の他企業の事業や営業権、さらには企業そのものを買い受けること。

TOB（株式の公開買い付け）
takeover bid
株式会社の経営権取得などを目的に、買い付け期間や買い取り株数、買い取り価格を公表して、不特定多数の株主から株式市場外で株式を買い集める制度。

ハゲタカファンド
buy-out fund
企業買収によって、高利回りを得ることを目的としたファンド。複数の投資家から集めた資金を買収対象の企業に投資して経営に関与し、企業価値を高めてから売却する手法をとることが多い。また、主に買収先の資産やキャッシュフローを担保とした借入で資金を調達する。

自己資本比率
equity ratio
☞ 2日目

ROE（自己資本利益率）
return on equity
企業が株主から預かった資金をもとに、どの程度の利益を生み出したかを示す指標。
〔ROE ＝純利益÷自己資本〕

純利益
net income
☞ 4日目

TRANSLATION

小浜教授：さて、買収の話も、実際の例を引いて考えてみよう。アメリカ系のスティール・パートナーズというファンドがブルドックソースに TOB（株式の公開買い付け）を行った案件は、大きく報道されたから知ってるね。ブルドックソースはなぜ、狙われたんだろうか？

マキ：会社を買収するってことは、その会社の株主になることですよね。株主になることで儲かるためには、例えば、その会社の資産を高く切り売りして利益を上げるとか、その会社を欲しがっている別の会社に自分の持っている株を高く売却するとか――そうできる可能性が高いってこと？

小浜：おっ、まるでハゲタカファンドのマネジャーの発想だね。それはそれで重要な考え方なんだけど、ここでは、貸借対照表との関係から考えてみよう。自己資本比率が高くて、ROE が低い会社がよく狙い撃ちされるんだ。

マキ：ROE？ ROE って何ですか？

小浜：ROE は return on equity の略称で、純利益を純資産で割った数字なんだ。ROA とどこが違うか分かるかな？

マキ：ROA を算出するときに使ったのは営業利益だけど、ROE の場合は純利益ですね。どうして違う利益を使うんですか？

小浜：よく違いに気が付いたね。この違いはものすごく大事なんだ。ROE の計算に純利益を使うのは、ROE が、株主から預かっている資金に対する利益率を計算するものだからさ。利益にもいろいろあるけど、株主に帰属する利益は、税金（所得税）を支払った後の純

income tax.

Maki: I see. ROE is the figure you get when you divide net income by net assets. So, if the net assets amount is small, I mean, if the equity ratio is low, will ROE be high?

Obama: Yes, it will. Conversely, if the equity ratio is high, the ROE will be low. The low ROE means that the return to shareholders is low, and the stock price of a company with low ROE will stay at a low level. Companies with a low stock price tend to become targets for purchase. In addition, if the company's equity ratio is high, it means that the company is financially stable and its cash flow is also likely to be stable. This type of company often has hidden assets such as land, and so it's a perfect target for a buy-out fund.

Maki: Oh, I see. I thought that the higher the equity ratio, the more stable the company, but from a different perspective, this type of company is very good prey for a buy-out fund.

Obama: It's a sitting duck, isn't it?

自己資本比率が低いほどROEは上がる

①balance sheet
①貸借対照表

assets 100 資産	liabilities 50 負債
	net assets 50 純資産

②balance sheet
②貸借対照表

assets 100 資産	liabilities 90 負債
	net assets 10 純資産

● どちらも純利益を10とした場合

	①	②
return on assets (net profit base) ROA（純利益ベース）	10%	10%
return on equity ROE	20%	100%

負債が大きいとROEが高くなる

KEYWORDS

含み益
hidden assets / unrealized gains

貸借対照表上に記載されている有価証券や土地などの時価（評価額）が、それらを購入または取得した時の金額よりも高い状態のこと。または、それらを時価で売却したり、評価替えしたりした場合に発生するであろう利益。

利益でなくちゃいけない。

マキ：なるほど。じゃあ、ROEは純利益を純資産で割った数字だから、純資産が少ない場合、つまり、自己資本比率が低い場合にはROEは上がるってことですか？

小浜：そうなるね。だから逆に、自己資本比率が高いとROEは下がる。ROEが低いということは、株主に対するリターンが少ないということだから、ROEが低い会社は株価が低迷する。株価が低い会社は当然、買収の対象になりやすい。しかも、自己資本比率が高い会社は、財務的に安定していて、キャッシュフローも安定していることが期待できるし、そうした会社に限って、土地などの含み益があることも多いから、ハゲタカファンドにとっては絶好のターゲットになる。

マキ：そういうことか。さっきは自己資本比率が高ければ高いほど会社の安定性が増すと思ったけど、見方を変えると、そういう会社はいい餌食になるってことですね。

小浜：鴨がネギ背負ってるってやつだね。

Words & Phrases   ①②③……は、その語が登場した行数を表しています。

- ① attempted　計画された
- ① actual　実際の
- ⑤ target　～を標的にする
- ⑧ likely to　～しそうである
- ⑰ stands for　（略語などが）～を表す
- ㉒ notice　気が付く
- ㉖ attributed to　～に帰属する、～によるものとする
- ㉛ Conversely,　反対に、逆に言えば
- ㊳ hidden　隠された、秘密の
- ㊶ perspective　ものの見方、観点
- ㊷ prey　餌食、被害者
- ㊸ sitting duck　攻撃しやすい獲物、無防備な人

Chapter 1

自己資本率の高い会社が狙われる理由

Maki: I'm learning a lot today, but I'm at a bit of a loss since there are so many figures. There are so many indexes. Which one do you think is most important in terms of management?

Prof. Obama: Good question! Well, I think it's ROA, although there are many people who disagree and think ROE is most important. But ROE can be increased by increasing ROA and by increasing financial leverage.

Maki: Is that so? Then, ROA is more important than ROE. Just a minute, though, what is financial leverage?

Obama: It's the figure you get when you divide total assets by net assets. Leverage is a lever. In finance, it means liabilities, in particular, liabilities with interest. Even if it's only a small amount of money, the lever can be very effective using liabilities with interest.

Maki: Well, I know that to get the equity ratio you divide net assets by total assets. So, does that mean that financial leverage is the reciprocal of the equity ratio?

Obama: That's right. In other words, if the financial leverage is high, then the equity ratio is low. Therefore, in this case, even if the net income is the same, ROE will be higher.

Maki: Really? That's not easy to understand. The equity ratio is a very important figure because it shows financial stability in the mid- or long-term, while the lower the equity ratio, the higher the ROE with the same net income. Isn't that strange?

Obama: It is strange. In short, it's quite important to increase ROE in terms of stock price policy. But, if you want to realize a high-

KEYWORDS

ROA（資産利益率）
return on assets
☞ 4日目

ROE（自己資本利益率）
return on equity
☞ 5日目

財務レバレッジ
financial leverage
資産を純資産で割った数字。自己資本比率（純資産÷資産）の逆数。会計の世界では、負債の中でも特に有利子負債のことを指す。

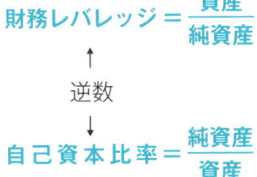

有利子負債
liabilities with interest
☞ 3日目、4日目

TRANSLATION

マキ：なんだか、今日1日でいろいろなことを勉強してますよね。これだけたくさん数字があると、分かんなくなっちゃいます。たくさんの指標が出てきましたけど、結局のところ、経営の指標として最も重視しなければならないのはどれなんですか？

小浜教授：いい質問だね。私に言わせればROAだ。ROEが一番大切だと思い違いをしている人が多いんだけどね。しかしROEは、ROAを高めることによって、また財務レバレッジを高めることによって上がる。

マキ：そうなんですか。じゃあ、ROEよりもROAが重要ですね。あれ、ちょっと待ってください。財務レバレッジって何ですか？

小浜：資産を純資産で割った数字さ。レバレッジというのは「てこ」のことなんだけど、ファイナンスの世界では、負債、特に「有利子負債」のことを言う。小さな資金でも、有利子負債を使えば、てこの原理で大きな力が出せるんだよ。

マキ：あれ？ 自己資本比率を算出するには、純資産を資産で割るんですよね。じゃあ、財務レバレッジというのは自己資本比率の逆数ってこと？

小浜：その通り。つまり、財務レバレッジが高いということは、自己資本比率が低いということ。そうなれば、同じ純利益を出しても、ROEは高くなる。

マキ：えっ？ ちょっと分かんないです。自己資本比率は、中長期的な財務安定性を表す大事な数字でしたよね。でも、それを低めれば低めるほど、同じ純利益でもROEを高めることができる。これって何かおかしくないですか？

小浜：確かにおかしいね。要するに、ROEを高めることは、株価対策として大切なんだ。しかしそれを、財務レバ

er ROE by increasing the financial leverage, it will cause problems with financial stability. So, what you need to do is to increase ROA before increasing ROE, which is to say that ROA is more important.

Maki: Well, it sounds very good in theory, but does it work in practice?

Obama: Yes, it does. A company finances the money to secure assets by both liabilities and net assets. In terms of management philosophy, by increasing the ROA a company becomes responsible for producing the return to match both its liability and its net assets. In this sense, this philosophy is superior to the philosophy of merely increasing ROE to match net assets.

Maki: In other words, managers need to respect the banks that offer loans and customers who buy corporate bonds.

Obama: That's right. Recently, American style management that places its greatest emphasis on shareholders is rampant. But, making shareholders the top priority leads to unethical management and unethical business practices. We've already seen such businesses fail with our own eyes!

ＲＯＡとＲＯＥの関係

$$ROA = \frac{純利益}{資産} = \frac{純利益}{売上高} \times \frac{売上高}{資産}$$

$$= （売上高利益率）\times（資産回転率）$$

$$ROE = \frac{純利益}{純資産} = \frac{純利益}{売上高} \times \frac{売上高}{資産} \times \frac{資産}{純資産}$$

$$= （ROA）\times（財務レバレッジ）$$

より大切なのはＲＯＡ

KEYWORDS

融資
loan
金融機関が、企業や個人などに有利子で金銭を貸し出すこと。ローン、借金。融資は、貸し手側には債権（資産）、借り手側には債務（負債）となり、貸し手側を債権者、借り手側を債務者と呼ぶ。

社債
corporate bond
企業が債券を発行して、市場から資金を調達する手法。直接金融と呼ばれる。なお、bondは債券の総称。

レッジを高めることで実現しようとすれば、今度は財務安定性の観点からは問題が生じる。つまり、やらなければならないのは、ROEを高める以前に、まずはROAを高めることであり、すなわちROAの方がROEより重要だ、ということだ。

マキ：何か、理論的にはすごくよさそうですけど、実際にそうなるんですか？

小浜：ああ、なるとも。資産を賄うために、会社は、負債と純資産の両方で資金を調達する。経営哲学の立場から言うと、ROAを上げるというのは、負債と純資産の両方に対してそれに見合ったリターンを出す責務があるという考え方を示していて、これは、純資産だけに見合ったリターンであるROEさえ出していればよいという考え方に優先する。

マキ：つまり企業の経営者は、融資を提供してくれる銀行や、社債を購入してくれる債権者も大切にしなくちゃいけないってことですね。

小浜：その通り。最近は株主を偏重するアメリカ型経営が横行しているが、その株主さえ満足させておけばいいという考えは、倫理なき経営、倫理なきビジネス手法の温床となり得る。そして、そのようなビジネスが破綻した事実を、われわれは目の当たりにしているじゃないか！

Words & Phrases

①②③……は、その語が登場した行数を表しています。

- ① at a loss　途方に暮れて
- ⑤ disagree　異議を唱える
- ⑪ lever　てこ、てこ棒
- ⑰ reciprocal　逆数
- ㉒ stability　安定性。financial stabilityで「財務安定性」
- ㉖ realize　実現する
- ㉗ cause　引き起こす
- ㉙ which is to say　つまり
- ㉛ in theory　理論的には、理論上は
- ㉛ work　（目的通りに）機能する
- ㉛ in practice　現実面では
- ㉟ philosophy　哲学、根本原理
- ㊲ superior to　〜よりも優れている
- ㊴ respect　尊重する、顧慮する
- ㊷ place　置く
- ㊷ emphasis　重要性、強調
- ㊷ rampant　まん延した、広がった
- ㊸ leads to　〜につながる
- ㊹ unethical　倫理に反する、非道徳的な
- ㊹ business practice　ビジネス手法

Chapter 1

7日目 なぜ、イオンはダイエーを子会社にしないのか？

TR08

Maki: Please tell me one last thing, Prof. Obama. You told me earlier that you'd explain about consolidation in detail.

Prof. Obama: Oh, yes. In Japan, it has become obligatory from the fiscal year that ended March 2000 to disclose **consolidated financial statements.** It now plays a more important role than the unconsolidated financial statements of one company.

Maki: Does that mean that a company's settlements of account must be made with those of the parent company?

Obama: Roughly speaking, yes, it does. There are so many terms that may easily be confused, such as a **subsidiary,** a group company, an **affiliated company** and a **subcontractor.** I'd like to check how well you know them before we continue. Can you tell me what a subsidiary is?

Maki: Is it a company whose shares are owned by a parent company?

Obama: Yes, but how about the percentage?

Maki: Oh, it's determined by the percentage!

Obama: Yes, it's the accounting principle called **"equity method"** that defines a subsidiary. In Japan, if a parent company has more than 50%* of the shares of another company, that company becomes a subsidiary of the parent company and must be included in the parent company's consolidated accounts. If a parent company has less than 50%* of the shares of its group company, that company is an affiliated company and is distinguished from a subsidiary. And a subcontractor is a company that is contracted to work for the parent company regardless of

* CDでは誤って20%と読まれています。

KEYWORDS

連結財務諸表
consolidated financial statements

実質的に支配従属関係にあるが、法的には独立した複数の企業からなるグループ（親会社・子会社）を1つの企業と見立てて、その経営成績・財務状況を示すもの。日本では2000年3月期から、連結中心での財務諸表開示が義務付けられた。

子会社
subsidiary

親会社に50％超の株式を保有されている等、実質的に支配されている企業のこと。子会社は、原則として親会社の連結決算対象となる。

関連会社
affiliated company

親会社が子会社以外で20％以上の株式を保有している等、経営に重要な影響を及ぼせる会社。原則として、持分法を適用して利益（損失）が連結決算に取り込まれる。

下請け企業
subcontractor

親会社から仕事を発注され、業務を請け負っている会社。「株式の保有」については関係がない。

持分法
equity method

連結財務諸表の様式や作成に関する会計規則で、有価証券の評価方法の1つ。

TRANSLATION

マキ：先生、最後に1つだけ教えてください。さっき、連結については後で詳しくって言われましたけど。

小浜教授：そうだったな。日本では2000年の3月期決算から、連結財務諸表が開示対象となって、企業単体の個別の財務諸表よりも、重要な役割を果たすようになった。

マキ：会社の決算を、親会社の決算と一緒にするってことですか？

小浜：ざっくり言えばそういうことだな。会社には子会社、グループ会社、関連会社、下請け企業などいろいろな名称があって、実に紛らわしい。話を続ける前に、それらを確認しておこう。子会社って何か説明できるかい？

マキ：親会社に株を保有されている会社のことでしょう？

小浜：そうだ。で、そのパーセントは？

マキ：あっ、その比率で決まるんだ！

小浜：そう。持分法という会計上の規則があって、それによって（連結対象となる）子会社が定められている。日本では現在、親会社が50％以上の株式を保有している場合に、その会社は子会社となり、親会社の連結決算の対象となる。50％以下を保有しているグループ会社のことは、関連会社と言って、子会社とは区別する。ちなみに、下請け企業というのは、親会社による株式の保有とは関係なく、親会社から仕事を請け負っている会社という意味さ。

マキ：それじゃ、親会社が儲かっていて

the ownership of shares by the parent company.

Maki: So, if a parent company is making a lot of profit and has a lot of money, does it change its affiliated companies to subsidiaries?

Obama: Not necessarily. For example, Aeon made Daiei an affiliated company—its percentage of shares in Daiei is up to 15%—but it hasn't made Daiei a subsidiary yet. Daiei was in a state of insolvency before bankruptcy and had a vast amount of interest-bearing liquidity which exceeded its net sales.

Maki: So, if a parent company makes another company a subsidiary, the parent company has to take responsibility for the subsidiary's liabilities with interest.

Obama: That's right. Daiei's liabilities with interest have been drastically reduced due to the debt relief granted by the Industrial Revitalization Corporation of Japan. If the parent company, Aeon, had made Daiei a subsidiary, they would have had to include Daiei's liabilities with interest in their consolidated accounts. Then, Aeon's equity ratio would have had to be lowered. However, although Aeon did not make Daiei a subsidiary, Aeon could implement their sales strategies by joint procurement and sharing of their systems and data.

Maki: That means we can make an educated guess about a company's strategies by learning how to read balance sheets. Thank you very much for your lecture. I've learned a lot today.

KEYWORDS

債務免除
debt relief
債権者の意思で債務をなかったものにする行為で、債権者の側から見ると債権放棄に当たる。平たく言うと、借金を棒引きにすること。

販売戦略
sales strategy
中・長期期間における販売活動の方向性、コンセプト。端的に言うと「どう取り組むか、何をすべきか」が strategy（戦略）であり、その戦略をどの方法で実践すべきか、というのが tactics（戦術）である。

お金があれば、関連会社をどんどん連結対象の子会社にしていくんですか？
小浜：必ずしもそうとは限らない。例えば、イオンはダイエーを傘下に加えたけれど、株式保有は15％に抑えて、ダイエーを子会社にはしないで、関連会社のままにしている。ダイエーは、破綻前には支払不能に陥っていて、売上高を超える有利子負債を抱えていたからね。
マキ：あ、ある会社を子会社にしたら、連結決算のときに、親会社はその子会社の有利子負債まで一緒にしなきゃいけなくなるんですね。
小浜：その通り。ダイエーの有利子負債は、産業再生機構の下で銀行の債務免除を受けて劇的に減少したけれど、それでももし、親会社となったイオンがダイエーを連結対象の子会社にしたならば、この有利子負債を合算しなければならなくなり、そうすると、イオンの自己資本比率は下がらざるを得なくなる。一方、イオンはダイエーを子会社にしなくても、仕入れの共通化や、システムやデータの共有ができれば、営業戦略的には目的を達成する。
マキ：要するに、貸借対照表の見方が分かれば、企業戦略の一端も読み解くことができるってわけですね。説明、ありがとうございました。今日はとても勉強になりました。

Words & Phrases   ①②③……は、その語が登場した行数を表しています。

- ② consolidation　連結、整理統合
- ③ obligatory　義務的な、必須の
- ⑦ settlement　清算、決済
- ⑨ term　ことば、専門用語
- ⑰ determine　決定する
- ⑲ define　定義する、特徴付ける
- ㉔ distinguish　区別する
- ㉖ contract　契約する
- ㉖ regardless of　～にかかわらず
- ㉞ insolvency　支払い不能、破産状態
- ㉞ vast　膨大な、巨額の
- ㉞ interest-bearing　利付き
- ㉟ net sales　生産高、売上高
- ㊴ drastically　大幅に、徹底的に
- ㊵ due to ～　～のために、おかげで
- ㊵ grant　許可する、与える
- ㊵ the Industrial Revitalization Corporation of Japan　（株式会社の）産業再生機構
- ㊻ implement　実行する、遂行する
- ㊻ joint procurement　共同購買
- ㊽ educated guess　知識や経験に基づく推測

Chapter 1

REVIEW EXERCISE

Chapter 1 で学んだ内容を復習しよう

TR09 まずは、チャンツのリズムに乗せて Keywords を発音しましょう。

- ☐ **liabilities**
  負債
- ☐ **balance sheet**
  貸借対照表
- ☐ **current assets**
  流動資産
- ☐ **current liabilities**
  流動負債

- ☐ **current ratio**
  流動比率
- ☐ **short-term liquidity**
  手元流動性
- ☐ **cash flow statement**
  キャッシュフロー計算書
- ☐ **financial statements**
  財務諸表

< pause >

- ☐ **net assets**
  純資産
- ☐ **equity ratio**
  自己資本比率
- ☐ **fixed assets**
  固定資産
- ☐ **consolidated balance sheets**
  連結貸借対照表

- ☐ **risk premium**
  リスクプレミアム
- ☐ **return on assets**
  資産利益率（ROA）
- ☐ **net income**
  （当期）純利益
- ☐ **buy-out**
  買収

< pause >

- ☐ **takeover bid**
  TOB（株式の公開買い付け）
- ☐ **return on equity**
  自己資本利益率（ROE）
- ☐ **hidden assets**
  含み益
- ☐ **financial leverage**
  財務レバレッジ

- ☐ **loan**
  融資
- ☐ **corporate bond**
  社債
- ☐ **subsidiary**
  子会社
- ☐ **affiliated company**
  関連会社

< pause >

- ☐ **subcontractor**
  下請け企業
- ☐ **equity method**
  持分法
- ☐ **stability**
  安定性、持続性
- ☐ **securities**
  有価証券、債権

- ☐ **operation**
  事業、運営
- ☐ **purchase**
  購入する、獲得する
- ☐ **trillion**
  兆
- ☐ **consolidation**
  連結、整理統合

会社の実力を英語で診断！

貸借対照表（英語版）を見ながら、以下の問いに答えましょう。

A社　Balance Sheet

Current assets	12,000	Current liabilities	11,000
Cash and deposits	2,000	Accounts payable	2,000
Marketable securities	500	Short-term borrowings	1,000
Inventories	1,800	Other current liabilities	8,000
Other current assets	7,700		
Fixed Assets	20,000	Long-term liabilities	8,000
Tangible fixed assets	8,000	Long-term debt	6,000
Other fixed assets	12,000	Other long-term liabilities	2,000
		Shareholders' equity	13,000
Total assets	32,000	Total liabilities and shareholders' equity	32,000

B社　Balance Sheet

Current assets	16,000	Current liabilities	18,000
Cash and deposits	2,000	Accounts payable	6,000
Marketable securities	0	Short-term borrowings	4,000
Inventories	4,000	Other current liabilities	8,000
Other current assets	10,000		
Fixed Assets	16,000	Long-term liabilities	8,000
Tangible fixed assets	8,000	Long-term debt	7,000
Other fixed assets	8,000	Other long-term liabilities	1,000
		Shareholders' equity	6,000
Total assets	32,000	Total liabilities and shareholders' equity	32,000

問1 会社の「短期的な財務安定性」を判断するには、貸借対照表のどの数値から分析しますか。代表的な2つの指標と、その計算方法を、英語と日本語で挙げてください。

指標①英（　　　　　）＝（　　　　　）／（　　　　　）
　　　日（　　　　　）＝（　　　　　）／（　　　　　）
指標②英（　　　　　）＝（　　　　　）／（　　　　　）
　　　日（　　　　　）＝（　　　　　）／（　　　　　）

問2 A社とB社は、どちらが「短期的な財務安定性」の点で優れていますか。問1で挙げた2つの指標それぞれについて、計算して答えましょう（損益計算書は79ページにあります）。
指標①A社：　　　　　　　　B社：
指標②A社：　　　　　　　　B社：

問3 問1の2つの指標のほかに、資金調達の点から、会社の「中長期的な財務安定性」を分析する指標と計算式を英語と日本語で答えて、AB両社について計算してください。
英（　　　　　）＝（　　　　　）／（　　　　　）A社：
日（　　　　　）＝（　　　　　）／（　　　　　）B社：

問4 会社の「利益率」を分析する上で使用する代表的な計算式を2つ日本語で示し、両社について計算してください。
①（　　　　　）＝（　　　　　）／（　　　　　）A社：＿＿＿＿　B社：＿＿＿＿
②（　　　　　）＝（　　　　　）／（　　　　　）A社：＿＿＿＿　B社：＿＿＿＿

● Chapter 1　8日目

解答と解説

A社　貸借対照表			
流動資産	12,000	流動負債	11,000
現金預金	2,000	買掛金	2,000
有価証券	500	短期借入金	1,000
棚卸資産	1,800	その他	8,000
その他	7,700		
固定資産	20,000	固定負債	8,000
有形固定資産	8,000	長期借入金	6,000
その他	12,000	その他	2,000
		純資産	13,000
資産合計	32,000	負債・純資産合計	32,000

B社　貸借対照表			
流動資産	16,000	流動負債	18,000
現金預金	2,000	買掛金	6,000
有価証券	0	短期借入金	4,000
棚卸資産	4,000	その他	8,000
その他	10,000		
固定資産	16,000	固定負債	8,000
有形固定資産	8,000	長期借入金	7,000
その他	8,000	その他	1,000
		純資産	6,000
資産合計	32,000	負債・純資産合計	32,000

問1 指標① current ratio = current assets ／ current liabilities
　　　　　　（流動比率）＝（流動資産）／（流動負債）
　　　指標② short-term liquidity =（cash and deposit + marketable securities）／ monthly sales
　　　　　　（手元流動性）＝（現金預金＋すぐに資金化できる有価証券等）／（平均月間売上）
　　　【解説】immediately salable securities（すぐに資金化できる有価証券）は、財務諸表では、marketable securities と呼ばれる。

問2 流動比率　A社：12,000 ÷ 11,000 ＝ 109.1%　○
　　　　　　　　B社：16,000 ÷ 18,000 ＝ 88.9%
　　　手元流動性　A社：(2,000+500) ÷ (26,000／12) ＝ 1.15月　○
　　　　　　　　　B社：2,000 ÷ (24,000／12) ＝ 1.00月
　　　【解説】流動比率と手元流動性が分からなければ、1日目を復習しよう。

問3 指標　equity ratio = net assets ／ total assets　　A社：40%
　　　　　（自己資本比率）＝（純資産）／（［総］資産）　B社：18%

問4 （資産利益率）＝（営業利益）／（資産）
　　　A社：2,500 ÷ 32,000 ＝ 7.8%　　B社：500 ÷ 32,000 ＝ 1.6%）
　　　（自己資本利益率）＝（当期純利益）／（自己資本）
　　　A社：1,600 ÷ 13,000 ＝ 12.3%　　B社：110 ÷ 6,000 ＝ 1.8%

Chapter 1 のまとめ

● 貸借対照表（balance sheet: B/S）とは……
ある1時点の会社の資産、負債、資本の内容を表す

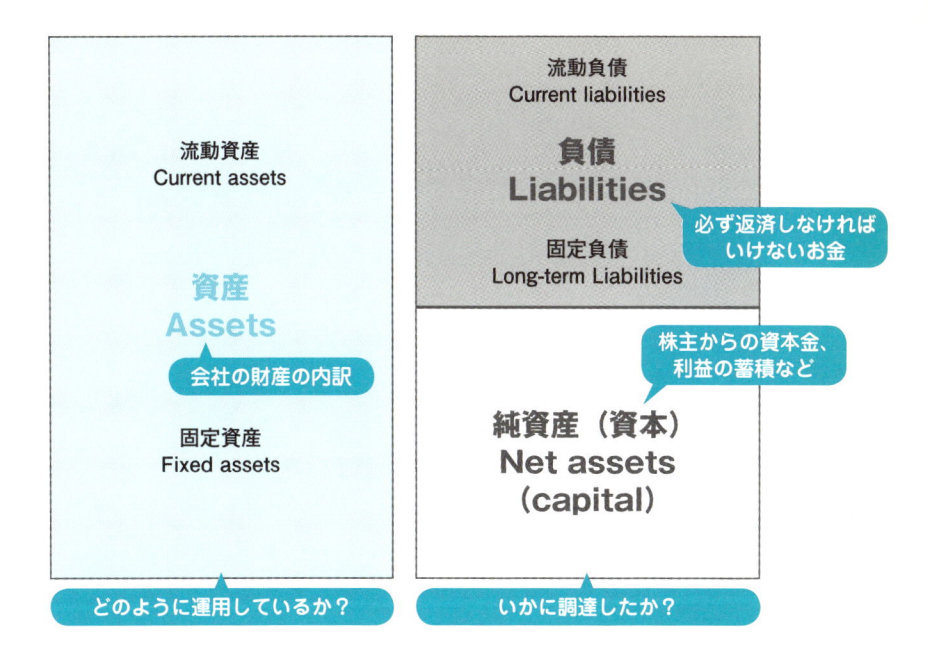

資産 Assets（会社の財産の内訳）	負債 Liabilities（必ず返済しなければいけないお金）
流動資産 Current assets	流動負債 Current liabilities
固定資産 Fixed assets	固定負債 Long-term Liabilities
	純資産（資本） Net assets (capital)（株主からの資本金、利益の蓄積など）
どのように運用しているか？	いかに調達したか？

● 下線部に対応する英語を記入しながら、学習内容を最後にまとめましょう。

貸借対照表の注目点！

流動比率＝（流動資産÷流動負債）が100％を超えているか？

手元流動性＝（現預金＋すぐに資金化できるもの）÷月商が1〜1.5カ月分あるか？

自己資本比率＝純資産÷資産が15〜20％以上あるか？

ROA（資産利益率＝利益÷資産）がWACC（加重平均資本調達コスト）を上回っているか？

ROE（自己資本利益率＝純利益÷自己資本）は健全な高さがあるか？

Column 1

経営的に理解できれば、ビジネスマンには十分！

　ビジネスマンが自分の仕事やキャリアに役立つようにと会計を勉強するとき、最初につまずくのが貸借対照表です。必要もないのに、会計を「会計的」に勉強するから嫌になるのですが、ここでいう「会計的に勉強」とは、貸借対照表の「作り方」や、「仕訳」などを勉強することを指しています。

　しかし、ビジネスマンは「経営的」に会計を理解すれば十分です。経理でも担当しない限り、貸借対照表や損益計算書といった財務諸表の「作り方」を知る必要はありません。なのに、そこからアプローチしようとするから、会計が分かりにくくなるのです。

　繰り返しますが、税理士や会計士になろうとか、経理を仕事で担当するとかでない限り、ビジネスマンにとって、財務諸表の「作り方」を知る必要はまずありません。これは、パソコンの作り方を学んでからパソコンの使い方を知る人などいないのと同じです。多くのビジネスマンにとっては、財務諸表を「経営的」にどう解釈すればよいかが分かればよいのであって、逆に下手に作り方などに深入りすると、「木を見て森を見ず」にもなりかねません。

（こみや かずよし）

＊ COLUMN 1〜4は、『「1秒！」で財務諸表を読む方法』（小宮一慶著／東洋経済新報社刊）からの転載です。

Chapter 2

国家財政が破綻しない不思議

ココを見て納得! ―損益計算書―

Chapter 2

9 損益計算書とは？

Maki: I've heard the Japanese government has a huge amount of loans. Is that true?

Prof. Obama: It sure is. In fact, the accumulated fiscal deficit of the Japanese government is over 800 trillion yen, if you count both long- and short-term loans.

Maki: Eight hundred trillion yen? Why doesn't the Japanese government go bankrupt, if it has such a huge deficit? If it were a company, it would have gone broke a long time ago, wouldn't it?

Obama: Yes, but to understand the reasons, you've got to understand what an "income statement" is.

Maki: An income statement? Oh, that's one of the three financial statements that you mentioned before. An income statement shows the "loss" and the "profit" of a company during a certain period, doesn't it?

Obama: Great! You can see what condition the Japanese government's fiscal account is in by comparing it with the income statement of a company. For example, let's look at the income statement of Nissan Motor Company.* Where do you look if you have only "one second"?

Maki: Well, that would be the "net sales", because it's directly connected with the net income.

Obama: Bingo! A company makes its net sales by selling goods and services to customers. So, the "net sales" figure shows the size of contact between the company and society. In other words, it represents the "presence" of the company in society.

KEYWORDS

財政赤字
fiscal deficit
国や自治体の抱える借金。「歳入＜歳出」となっている収支。歳入には、税収や公債発行によって得られる資金が含まれ、歳出には、公共投資や社会福祉・教育などの支出のほか、公債の元利払いが含まれる。
☞ 13日目

財務三表
three financial statements
貸借対照表と損益計算書にキャッシュフロー計算書を合わせた、3つの財務諸表の呼称。キャッシュフロー計算書は、日本では、2000年3月期から連結決算制度が始まった際に導入された。
☞ 2日目

売上高
net sales
会社が、商品やサービスを顧客に提供するなどした営業活動の対価として受け取る収入。企業の社会での存在を表すので、売上高が上がれば、社会での存在が増えたことになる。英式では turnover。

TRANSLATION

マキ：日本政府は巨額の借金を抱えているって聞いたことがあるんですけど、そうなんですか？

小浜教授：その通り。実は、日本政府が抱える財政赤字は、長期短期合わせると800兆円を超えているんだ。

マキ：800兆円?!　そんなにひどい赤字があるのに、どうして日本の財政は破綻しないんですか。企業だったらとっくに倒産していますよね？

小浜：うん。その謎を理解するには、まず「損益計算書」について理解しないといけないな。

マキ：損益計算書？　あ、前に先生が言っていた財務三表の1つですね。損益計算書は、企業のある期間の「損失」と「利益（儲け）」の状況を表したもの、ですよね！

小浜：やるじゃない！　日本の財政事情は、企業の損益計算書と比較することで、よく見えてくるんだ。じゃあ、実際に日産自動車の損益計算書*を見てみようか。どうだい、「1秒！」だけ見るとしたらどこを見る？

マキ：それはやっぱり「売上高」でしょう！純利益に直結するものですからね。

小浜：正解！　会社というのは、商品やサービスを顧客に提供して売ることで、売上高を受け取る。だから売上高は、その会社と社会との接点の大きさ、つまり、その企業の社会での「プレゼンス（存在）」を表しているんだよ。

＊日産自動車の損益計算書（平成19年3月期）は、52－53ページを参照。

● Chapter 2　9日目

Maki: Then, if the net sales go up, the presence of the company grows; and if the net sales go down, the presence shrinks. So then, we've got to see how much the net sales figure has increased or decreased by comparing it with the previous year's figure listed on the income statement.

Obama: So far, so good. Now, there's another important point when you see an increase and decrease in the net sales. Do you know about the assets turnover ratio?

Maki: Isn't that the index that shows how efficiently assets have been used? It's obtained by dividing net sales by total assets, isn't it?

Obama: Exactly! Now, let's look at the assets turnover ratio of Nissan. It was 0.82 in fiscal year 2005, and 0.84 in fiscal year 2006.

Maki: Oh, the turnover increased. So, Nissan improved its usage of total assets.

Obama: That's right. The key point in looking at the net sales is the relation between the increase and decrease of the total assets on the balance sheet, and the increase and decrease of the net sales on the income statement. If the increase ratio of the net sales is smaller than for the total assets, it tells you that the assets have been used less efficiently than before.

Maki: OK, I get it. We've got to check both the balance sheet and the income statement.

assets turnover ratio

$$\frac{\text{net sales}}{\text{assets}} = \text{assets turnover ratio}$$

Nissan's case: 0.82 (FY2006) →improved→ 0.84 (FY2007)

the higher, the better

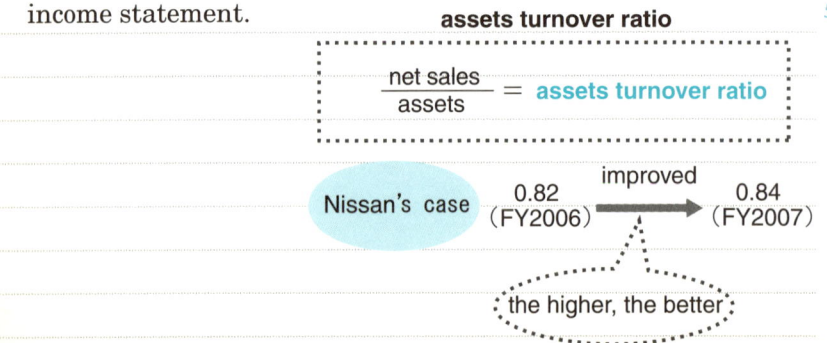

KEYWORDS

資産回転率
assets turnover ratio

資産の有効活用度合いを表す指標。売上高の伸び率が資産の伸び率より大きい場合が正常で、逆であれば資産の活用度合いが悪化していることを示す。

資産回転率

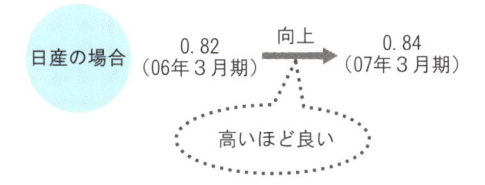

$$\frac{売上高}{資産} = 資産回転率$$

日産の場合　0.82（06年3月期）→向上→ 0.84（07年3月期）

高いほど良い

年度
fiscal year

1月から12月を1年とする暦とは別に、4月1日から翌年3月31日までのように適宜定められた会計や業務の期間。民間企業の場合は「事業年度」、国に関しては「会計年度」と呼ぶ。略語はＦＹで、英式では financial year。また、4月から3月末を年度としている場合、平成19年3月期が、平成18年度の決算期を指す。

マキ：つまり、売上高が上がればその企業の社会での存在が大きくなり、売上高が下がればその存在が小さくなった、ということですね。それじゃ、売上高は、損益計算書に載っている前年度分の数字と比較して、どのくらい増減したのかも見なくちゃいけませんね。

小浜：そこまではその通り。だけど、売上高の増減を見る上で大切なことがもうひとつある。「資産回転率」を知っているかね？

マキ：資産がどれだけ効率良く使われているかを表す指標で、確か「売上高÷資産」の数字じゃなかったでしたっけ？

小浜：その通り！　じゃあ、日産の資産回転率を見てみよう。2005年度が0.82で、2006年度が0.84……。

マキ：あ、回転率が上がっています。つまり日産は、資産の有効活用度合いが向上したってことですね！

小浜：そうなんだ。つまり、売上高を見る上で大切なのは、貸借対照表の資産の増減と、損益計算書の売上高の増減の関係に注意することなんだ。もしも売上高の伸び率が資産の伸び率より小さくなっていれば、それはつまり、資産の活用効率が前より落ちてしまった、ということさ。

マキ：なるほど。貸借対照表と損益計算書は、両方必ずチェック、ですね！

Words & Phrases
①②③……は、その語が登場した行数を表しています。

- ③ accumulated　累積した
- ④ trillion　1兆
- ⑧ go broke　倒産する、破綻する
- ㉒ connect　つなぐ、連結させる
- ㉓ Bingo!　正解！　その通り！
- ㉓ goods　商品、物品
- ㉔ figure　数字
- ㉕ contact　接点
- ㉖ represent　～を表す、～を示す
- ㉘ shrink　縮まる、小さくなる
- ㉜ so far　これまでのところ
- ㉟ index　指数、指標
- ㉟ efficiently　効果的に、効率良く
- ㊱ obtain　手に入れる、得る
- ㊳ Exactly.　まさにその通り
- ㊶ improve　改善する
- ㊾ have got to　～しなければならない

Nissan Motor Co.
Consolidated Statements of Income
(FY2006 and FY2005)
[in million of yen, ( ) indicates loss or minus]

The following information has been prepared in accordance with accounting principles generally accepted in Japan.

	FY2006	FY2005	Change Amount	%
	100%	100%		
Net sales	10,468,583	9,428,292	1,040,291	11.0%
Cost of sales	8,027,186	7,040,987	986,199	
	23.3%	25.3%	(2.0)%	
Gross profit	2,441,397	2,387,305	54,092	2.3%
SELLING, GENERAL AND ADMINISTRATIVE EXPENSES	1,664,458	1,515,464	148,994	
	7.4%	9.2%	(1.8)%	
Operating income	776,939	871,841	(94,902)	(10.9)%
NON-OPERATING INCOME	65,914	74,799	(8,885)	
Interest and dividend income	25,546	21,080	4,466	
Equity in earnings of unconsolidated subsidiaries & affiliates	20,187	37,049	(16,862)	
Foreign exchange gain	5,796	—	5,796	
Other non-operating income	14,385	16,670	(2,285)	
NON-OPERATING EXPENSES	81,802	100,768	(18,966)	
Interest expense	30,664	25,646	5,018	
Amortization of net retirement benefit obligation at transition	10,928	11,145	(217)	
Foreign exchange loss	—	34,836	(34,836)	
Other non-operating expenses	40,210	29,141	11,069	
	7.3%	9.0%	(1.7)%	
Ordinary income	761,051	845,872	(84,821)	(10.0)%
SPECIAL GAINS	73,687	82,455	(8,768)	
SPECIAL LOSSES	137,306	119,286	18,020	
	6.7%	8.6%	(1.9)%	
Income before income taxes and minority interests	697,432	809,041	(111,609)	(13.8)%
INCOME TAXES—CURRENT	202,328	274,463	(72,135)	
INCOME TAXES—DEFERRED	9,834	(20,055)	29,889	
MINORITY INTERESTS	24,474	36,583	(12,109)	
	4.4%	5.5%	(1.1)%	
Net Income	460,796	518,050	(57,254)	(11.1)%

日産自動車株式会社の連結損益計算書

（単位：百万円）

科目	平成18年度 (18/4～19/3)	平成17年度 (17/4～18/3)	対前年度 増減率
	100%	100%	
売上高	10,468,583	9,428,292	11.0%
売上原価	8,027,186	7,040,987	
	23.3%	25.3%	
売上総利益	2,441,397	2,387,305	2.3%
販売費及び一般管理費	1,664,458	1,515,464	
	7.4%	9.2%	
営業利益	776,939	871,841	△10.9%
営業外収益	65,914	74,799	
受取利息及び配当金	25,546	21,080	
持分法による投資利益	20,187	37,049	
為替差益	5,796	−	
その他の営業外収益	14,385	16,670	
営業外費用	81,802	100,768	
支払利息	30,664	25,646	
退職給付会計基準変更時差異	10,928	11,145	
為替差損	−	34,836	
その他の営業外費用	40,210	29,141	
	7.3%	9.0%	
経常利益	761,051	845,872	△10.0%
特別利益	73,687	82,455	
特別損失	137,306	119,286	
	6.7%	8.6%	
税金等調整前当期純利益	697,432	809,041	△13.8%
法人税、住民税及び事業税	202,328	274,463	
法人税等調整額	9,834	△20,055	
少数株主利益	24,474	36,583	
	4.4%	5.5%	
当期純利益	460,796	518,050	△11.1%

Chapter 2

10日目 売上原価と製造原価の違い

Prof. Obama: By the way, on the income statement, "gross profit" and "cost of sales" are written under net sales. Do you understand those terms?

Maki: I think so. I get gross profit by subtracting cost of sales from net sales. And the cost of sales is the expense that was needed to make the products, isn't it?

Obama: So, what is the difference between "cost of sales" and "cost of production"?

Maki: Cost of production is the expense needed to make products. Oh, that's what I said for cost of sales.

Obama: OK, let's clear that up. Cost of production is literally "the expense needed to make products". On the other hand, cost of sales is the "cost of products that have actually been sold". That's an important difference.

Maki: But then, how about products that have been made but not sold? I don't think cost of production is listed in the income statement.

Obama: You noticed! Cost of production is listed in the inventory on the balance sheet. That is, it is listed as stock. All the expenses needed to make products are calculated as stock, and the products that are actually sold are calculated as cost of sales and are listed as expense. In other words, cost of products becomes inventory, and then the inventory becomes cost of sales.

So, even if there's a profit in the income statement, you have to check the inventory in the balance sheet. There could

KEYWORDS

売上総利益
gross profit

売上高から売上原価を引いたもの。いわゆる「粗利益」。ちなみに、売上総利益を売上高で割ったものが売上総利益率（粗利率）。一般に、製造業では売上総利益率は低い傾向がある。

売上原価
cost of sales

損益計算書で損益を計算する際に用いられる原価で、１年間に製造した製品にかかった費用のうち、売れた分だけの製造原価。

製造原価
cost of production

１年間に製造した製品にかかった費用。具体的には、原材料費・労務費・製造間接費など。売れた分だけが売上原価として費用に計上され、まだ売れていない製品の製造原価は、費用ではなく、棚卸資産（在庫）として計上される。

棚卸資産
inventory

仕入れ商品や、製造した製品のうち、売れ残って在庫となっている分。売上高が下落し棚卸資産が増加していれば、不良在庫の可能性がある。

TRANSLATION

小浜教授：ところで、損益計算書では売上高の下に「売上総利益」や「売上原価」と書かれているけど、これらの言葉の意味がちゃんと分かっているかな？

マキ：たぶん、分かってます。売上総利益は売上高から売上原価を引いたものですよね。で、売上原価は製品を作るのにかかった費用のこと、ですよね？

小浜：じゃあ、「売上原価」と「製造原価」はどう違うの？

マキ：製造原価は、製品を作るのにかかった費用のこと。あれ？　売上原価のときと同じこと言ってますね。

小浜：じゃあ、整理しておこう。製造原価は文字通り「製品を作るのにかかった費用」のこと。それに対して売上原価は、製品が「実際に売れた分だけの製造原価」のこと。この違いはとても大切なんだ。

マキ：でも、じゃあ、作ったけど売れ残っている製品はどうなっているんですか？　製造原価なんて項目、損益計算書には記載されてないですよね。

小浜：よく気が付いたね。製造原価は、貸借対照表の棚卸資産に計上されている。つまり、在庫として計上されているんだ。作るのにかかった費用はいったん、すべてその期の在庫になる。そして、そこから売れた分だけが売上原価として計上されて費用になる。つまり、製造原価→棚卸資産→売上原価、となるわけだ。

　だから、損益計算書上は利益が出ていたとしても、貸借対照表の棚卸資産を必ずチェックしなければならないん

be a huge amount of "dead stock" in inventory. In fact, Nissan's inventory has increased by 17.3% from March 31, 2006 to March 31, 2007. This increase is a lot bigger than the increase in the net sales.

Maki: In other words, the increase in the net sales doesn't necessarily mean an improvement in management. After all, it's important to compare both the balance sheet and the income statement.

Obama: It surely is. There's another thing you've got to keep an eye on regarding cost of sales, and that's the cost of sales ratio. The cost of sales ratio is the figure you get when you divide cost of sales by net sales. We need to see whether the ratio has increased or not.

Maki: If the ratio has increased, it means that the percentage of the cost of sales in the net sales got bigger because of increased cost of production or increased purchase price; which also means that the profit has decreased. Nissan's cost of sales ratio is calculated at 74.4% in the fiscal year ended March 2006 and at 76.7% in the fiscal year ended March 2007. So it's risen by over 2%.

Obama: Now, let's compare the gross profit. The gross profit has surely become larger. But, the gross profit increase rate was 2.3% in the fiscal year ended March 2007—not much compared to the net sales increase rate of 11% in the same period. That shows that the increase in the cost of sales ratio has had a big effect.

① cost of raw materials
② cost of labor
③ manufacturing overhead cost

cost of production

cost of purchase

inventory (stock)

cost of sales

KEYWORDS

不良在庫
dead stock

売れる見込みのない良くない在庫のこと。売れていない商品や回転の悪い商品に加えて、不良品や期限切れの商品も含む。

売上原価率
cost of sales ratio

作った製品にかかった費用のうち、売れた分だけの製造原価の比率。この比率が上昇していれば、製造コストや仕入れの上昇、すなわち儲けの減少を意味する。

〔売上原価率＝売上原価÷売上高〕

製造原価と売上原価

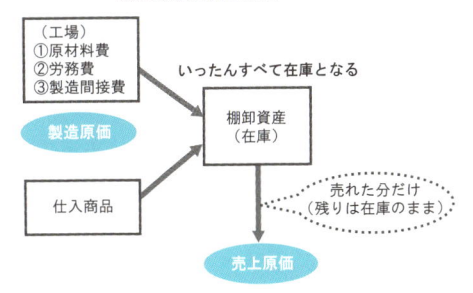

（工場）
①原材料費
②労務費
③製造間接費
→ 製造原価
→ いったんすべて在庫となる
→ 棚卸資産（在庫）
仕入商品 →
（売れた分だけ（残りは在庫のまま））
→ 売上原価

だ。棚卸資産に「不良在庫」がたまっている可能性があるからね。事実、日産の場合も、平成18年（2006年）3月期から平成19年（2007年）3月期にかけて、棚卸資産が17.3％増えている。これは、売上高の伸び率よりずいぶん大きいよね。

マキ：つまり、売上高が伸びても、それだけで経営状態がよくなったとは言えない。やっぱり、貸借対照表と損益計算書、両方の比較が大事なんですね。

小浜：そうだ。売上原価に関係して注意しておかないといけない重要なことがもうひとつある。それは、売上原価率だ。この売上原価率の数字、すなわち「売上原価÷売上高」が上がっていないかどうか、注意していないといけなんだ。

マキ：売上原価率が上がっているということは、製造コストや仕入れの費用が増えたせいで、売上高に占める売上原価の割合が大きくなった、つまり、儲けが減ってしまった、ということですね。日産で売上原価率を計算してみると、平成18年（2006年）3月度が74.4％で、平成19年（2007年）3月度が76.7％。2％以上も上昇してますね。

小浜：ここで、売上総利益と見比べてみよう。売上総利益（の金額）は確かに大きくなっている。でも、平成19年（2007年）3月度の伸び率は2.3％。同時期の売上高の伸び率11.0％に比べると、これはかなり小さいよね。売上原価率の上昇がいかに響いてるかを示しているわけだ。

Words & Phrases

①②③……は、その語が登場した行数を表しています。

- ③ term　用語、専門語
- ④ subtract ～ from　……から～を引く
- ⑤ expense　費用、支出
- ⑥ product　製品、生産物
- ⑪ clear up　解決する、はっきりさせる
- ⑪ literally　文字通りに
- ⑲ stock　在庫
- ㉛ in other words　言い換えると
- ㉛ not necessarily　必ずしも～ない
- ㉝ compare　比べる、比較する
- ㉟ keep an eye on　～から目を離さない、注目する

Chapter 2

11日目 利益の種類と販売費および一般管理費

Maki: Professor Obama when I look at the income statement, I see a lot of terms with the word "profit", like "gross profit", "operating profit", "ordinary profit", and "net profit". How are they different?

Prof. Obama: You can understand the differences if you get the proper meaning of each term. Take "gross profit"—you get it by subtracting cost of sales from net sales. It can be used to see the percentage of the cost of sales in the net sales. Then, how about "operating profit"?

Maki: Operating profit is calculated by subtracting "selling and general administrative expenses" from gross profit. And, ordinary profit is calculated by subtracting "non-operating income and expenses" from operating profit.

Obama: So, what do you think "selling and general administrative expenses" means?

Maki: I know selling expenses are the expenses related to net sales, but … well, the general administrative expenses …

Obama: Those are the expenses that aren't directly related to production or purchasing. Selling expenses are expenses used for selling activities, as you said before. Advertising expenses are the main expenses. General administrative expenses are expenses used for the operation and administration of the company as a whole.

Maki: You mean the utilities expenses like electricity, gas and water?

Obama: Yes, and personnel and office expenses. Even if you make a

Keywords

営業利益
operating profit
売上総利益から「販売費及び一般管理費」を引いた利益。企業の本業での儲けを示す指標。＝ operating income。

経常利益
ordinary profit
営業利益を元に、金利などの営業外損益を調整して算出される利益。通称「ケイツネ」。

当期純利益
net profit
特別損益の調整により計算された利益から、税金を差し引き、税効果会計による税金の調整処理を行ったうえで計上される利益。

販売費及び一般管理費
selling and general administrative expenses
企業が本業の活動に要した費用のうち、製造や仕入れに直接関係のない費用。略称は「販管費」。販売手数料や販売促進費などの販売費と、操業所運営費、人件費、その他経費などの一般管理費からなる。

Translation

マキ：小浜先生、損益計算書を見ていると、「売上総利益」「営業利益」「経常利益」「当期純利益」と「利益」の付く用語がたくさんあるんですけど、それぞれ何が違うんですか？

小浜教授：その違いは、それぞれの言葉の意味をきちんと理解すれば分かる。例えば、「売上総利益」は、売上高から売上原価を引いたもので、売上高に占める売上原価の割合を見るのに使うよね。じゃあ、「営業利益」はどうだろう？

マキ：営業利益は、売上総利益から、「販売費及び一般管理費」を引いたもの。ついでに言うと経常利益は、営業利益から営業外損益を差し引いて計算したものですよね。

小浜：じゃあ、その「販売費及び一般管理費」って何なんだい？

マキ：販売費は売上高に関係した（販売にかかった）費用だとして、でも……一般管理費は、えーっと……

小浜：製造や仕入れとは直接関係のない費用のことなんだ。販売費は君の言った通り、販売活動にかかった費用のこと。広告宣伝費がその代表だな。一般管理費とは、企業全体を運営して管理するために要した費用のことだよ。

マキ：例えば、公共料金の光熱費とか水道代とかですか？

小浜：そう。あとは（製造に直接関係しない）人件費とか、事務所経費とかね。

good gross profit, you can't get an operating profit if there's a greater amount of selling and general administrative expenses. So, the **"selling and administrative expenses ratio"** is an important figure.

経常利益の算出法	
売上高	net sales
− 売上原価	cost of sales
売上総利益	gross profit
− 販売費及び一般管理費	selling and general administrative expenses
営業利益	operating profit
− 営業外損益	non-operating income and expenses
経常利益	ordinary profit

KEYWORDS

販管費率
selling and (general) administrative expenses ratio

売上高に対する「販売費及び一般管理費」の比率。粗利益が上昇していても、販管費率が高ければ利益は出ない。
〔販管費率＝販管費÷売上高〕

せっかく粗利益を稼いでも、販管費でそれを食われていては、営業利益は出ない。だから、「販管費率」も、重要な数字なんだ。

Words & Phrases　①②③……は、その語が登場した行数を表しています。

- ⑥ take　～を例として挙げる
- ⑱ production　製造
- ⑲ purchasing　購買、購入、仕入れ
- ⑳ advertising　広告に関する、広告の
- ㉔ utilities　公共料金
- ㉖ personnel expense　人件費
- ㉚ figure　数字

Chapter 2

12日目 当期純利益の算出方法とさまざまな損益

Prof. Obama: Now, what's "non-operating profit and loss"? This is the adjustment factor when you calculate ordinary profit out of operating profit.

Maki: Literally speaking, is it the profit or loss that comes from factors other than selling? Such as dividends, for example?

Obama: Exactly! As another example, interest payments are also included. The profit and loss that is due to exchange rate fluctuations caused by a "strong yen" or "weak yen" is also included here.

Maki: So, if you have to pay a lot of interest because you have large liabilities, a large amount is deducted from the operating profit. In the last lecture, you said that the equity ratio would be lowered if there were a large amount of liabilities with interest. So, if the liabilities with interest increase, the non-operating loss will also increase. This is so complex!

Obama: Yes, but I think you're getting the hang of it. Lastly, let's check the "net profit". Do you know how to calculate that?

Maki: I remember that we can get it by adjusting special gains and losses from the ordinary profit. But, I don't get what "special gains" and "special losses" really mean.

Obama: Special gains and special losses are the gains and losses that "happen one time only" or are "not ordinary". For example, you get a profit by selling a factory because it's been sold for more than its book value, or you make a loss by selling a subsidiary for less than its book value. They are the gains and losses that are produced specially on those occasions.

KEYWORDS

営業外損益
non-operating profit and loss

配当金・受取利息などの収益や、金利支払いなどの損益といった、企業の本業以外の活動から経常的に発生する収益を指す。

特別利益
special gains / extraordinary gains

一過性の利益。例えば、工場を売却して簿価より高く売れた場合の利益など、経常的ではなく、そのときだけ特別に生じる利益。

特別損失
special losses / extraordinary losses

一過性の損失。例えば、子会社を売却したら損失が出たというような場合など、経常的ではなく、そのときだけ特別に生じる損失。「特別」に special を用いるのは従来の日本方式で、国際会計基準となりつつある米国式では extraordinary を用いる。

TRANSLATION

小浜教授：じゃあ、「営業外損益」って何だい？　営業利益から経常利益を出すときに調整される要素なんだけど。

マキ：文字で考えると、営業以外の（営業と関係ない）部分から出た損益ってことですか？　例えば、配当金とか？

小浜：お、その通り！　ほかの例だと、金利の支払いもそうだし、「円高」や「円安」といった為替の変動から生じる損益もここに含まれる。

マキ：つまり、負債が多くて金利の支払いが多いと、その分をたくさん営業利益から引かれてしまう、ということですね。この前は（WACCの高い企業の場合）、有利子負債が増えると自己資本比率が下がってよい、という話でしたけど、今度は、有利子負債が増えすぎても営業外損益が増えてしまうなんて。難しいですね。

小浜：しっかり復習できているねえ！　最後に「当期純利益」について確認しよう。これはどうやって算出するのかな？

マキ：経常利益から特別利益や特別損失を調整して算出する、って習いました。だけど、肝心の「特別利益」と「特別損失」の意味がよく分からないです。

小浜：特別利益、特別損失というのは「一過性の」「経常的ではない」利益とか損失のことだ。例えば、工場を売却したら帳簿価格より高く売れて利益が出たとか、子会社を売却したら帳簿価格より安くて損失が出た、というように、その時だけ特別に生じた損益のことさ。

Maki: Now I understand. If I compare these to our household accounts, they are the extraordinary expenses that are incurred when we buy a house or the income earned when we sell a car. I have a clearer picture of the activities of a company now.

Obama: If you deduct the tax after adjusting special gains and losses out of the ordinary profit, you get the net profit. As a matter of fact, this "tax adjustment" is very important, and it's made based on "tax effect accounting". It's very complex, so for now, just remember the term. Now, we'll take a look at the fiscal accounts of the Japanese government, using what we learned about the income statement.

Maki: Oh yeah, I'd forgotten that's what we were doing!

KEYWORDS

税効果会計
tax effect accounting

当期純利益を算出するために使われる財務上の会計処理。実際に支払う税額と、将来戻ってくる、もしくは支払う予定の税額とを調整し、財務会計上の理論的な税額を計算する。また、法人税のルールと会計のルールとの違いによる税金計上タイミングのズレを調整する。

マキ：それで分かりました。家計に例えるなら、家を買ったときに負担する臨時の出費や、車を売ったときに得る収入ってことですね。なんだか企業活動のイメージがわいてきました！

小浜：で、経常利益から、この特別損益を調整した後に税金を差し引くと、当期純利益が計上されるんだ。実は、この「税金の調整」も大変重要で「税効果会計」に基づいて行われるんだが、これはとても複雑なので、今は言葉を覚えておくだけにとどめよう。じゃあ今度は、損益計算書について学んだ知識を使って、日本の財政を考えてみようか。

マキ：あっ、いよいよ本題ですね！

Words & Phrases　①②③……は、その語が登場した行数を表しています。

- ② adjustment　修正、調整
- ⑤ dividend　配当（金）
- ⑦ fluctuation　変動、ばらつき
- ⑪ deduct　～を差し引く、控除する
- ⑮ complex　複雑な、込み入った
- ⑯ get the hang of　～のこつをつかむ、理解する
- ㉒ ordinary　普通の、ありふれた
- ㉔ book value　帳簿価額
- ㉖ occasion　出来事
- ㉗ household accounts　家計簿
- ㉘ extraordinary　特別な、臨時の
- ㉘ incur　負う、負担する

Chapter 2

13日目 日本の財政赤字と プライマリーバランス

Prof. Obama: Now, let's study the fiscal account of the Japanese government, based on the idea of an income statement. To solve the mystery of why the Japanese government, with such a huge fiscal deficit, doesn't go bankrupt, we need to think about "primary balance".

Maki: Primary balance? I've seen the term in the paper.

Obama: It's also called "fundamental fiscal balance". It's the balance after deducting government bond repayment and bond interest. Simply stated, it's the balance obtained by deducting ordinary expenditures from ordinary income, such as tax revenues.

Maki: It's like the operating profit in the case of a company then, isn't it?

Obama: That's it! And the Japanese government says it'll be even by the year 2011.

Maki: If it were a company, the operating profit would then be in the black. Well, I'm relieved to hear the government is trying to do something about the fiscal deficit.

Obama: Well, you shouldn't be relieved yet. You have to realize that behind the expression "Primary balance shall be even" there are some big problems.

Maki: Big problems? Like what?

Obama: The first problem is that the Japanese government is making plans but neglecting the interest payment and the bond repayment. The present situation is that the national bond issuance balance is already about 547 trillion yen; and the

KEYWORDS

財政赤字
fiscal deficit
☞ 9日目

プライマリーバランス／基礎的財政収支
primary balance / fundamental fiscal balance
国債などの元金支払いや利払いなどを除いた政府の収支。税収などの通常収入と通常支出との収支。この収支がゼロまたは黒字だと、公共サービスのための支出を税負担で賄えていることを意味する。

国債の元金払い
government bond repayment
金利分だけでなく、国債の元金分を償還すること。repayment は「返済、払い戻し」で、「債券の金利（払い）」は bond interest。

TRANSLATION

小浜教授：さあ、日本政府の財政事情を、損益計算書の考え方をベースに考えてみよう。あれほど巨大な財政赤字を抱えている日本政府がなぜ破綻しないのかという謎を解くためには、プライマリーバランスについて考えなければならない。

マキ：プライマリーバランス？　そういえば、新聞で見かけたことがあります。

小浜：プライマリーバランスというのは「基礎的財政収支」とも言われて、国債などの元金支払いや利払いなどを除いた収支のことを指す。簡単に言えば、通常的に入ってくる税収などの収入から、通常の支出を差し引いた収支、ということだね。

マキ：じゃあ、企業でいうと、営業利益みたいなものですね！

小浜：その通り！　で、日本政府はこれを 2011 年までに均衡させると言っているんだ。

マキ：企業でいうなら、営業黒字にしますってことですね。へえー、国も一応、財政赤字をなんとかしようと考えているんですね。ちょっと安心しました。

小浜：それが、まだ安心しちゃいけない。「プライマリーバランスを均衡させる」という言葉には、実は、大きな問題がいくつか隠されていることに気付かないと。

マキ：大きな問題？　例えばどんなことですか？

小浜：問題の 1 つ目は、政府が利払いや元金の返済を無視してプランを立てているということだ。現状では、公債の残高だけでも約 547 兆円、地方も合わ

long-term liabilities including local governments' bonds amount to 733 trillion yen, according to the finance ministry's forecast at the end of 2007.

Maki: Wow, that's enormous! So, even if the operating profit is in the black, the government still has to make enormous interest payments. If the interest is larger than the operating profit, the ordinary profit and the net profit will be in the red.

Obama: However, what is still more important is the cash flow.

Maki: Is that the cash flow mentioned in the cash flow statement?

Obama: Yes, the cash flow should be understood as the money flow or the money balance. Even if a company is making an operating profit, it will go bankrupt if it doesn't have the money for servicing debts such as loan repayments and interest payments. In other words, if it is short of cash flow, it will go bankrupt.

Maki: Is that what you call "bankruptcy with a profit"?

Obama: Yes. In the case of a company with a huge amount of loans compared with the net sales or the profit, it is quite likely to go bankrupt with a profit.

Maki: So, achieving an operating profit isn't enough. We have to plan when and how much to reduce the loans, don't we?

Obama: Exactly! But, there's still another problem.

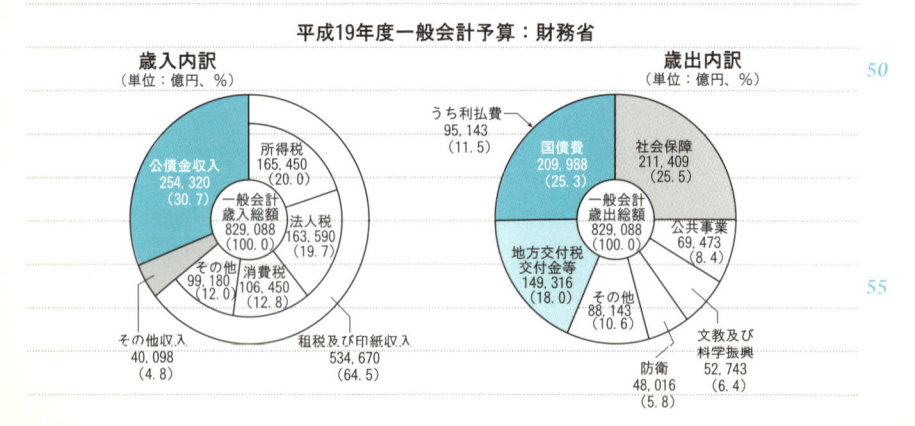

平成19年度一般会計予算：財務省

歳入内訳
（単位：億円、％）

公債金収入 254,320 (30.7)
所得税 165,450 (20.0)
一般会計歳入総額 829,088 (100.0)
法人税 163,590 (19.7)
消費税 106,450 (12.8)
その他 99,180 (12.0)
その他収入 40,098 (4.8)
租税及び印紙収入 534,670 (64.5)

歳出内訳
（単位：億円、％）

うち利払費 95,143 (11.5)
国債費 209,988 (25.3)
社会保障 211,409 (25.5)
一般会計歳出総額 829,088 (100.0)
公共事業 69,473 (8.4)
地方交付税交付金等 149,316 (18.0)
その他 88,143 (10.6)
防衛 48,016 (5.8)
文教及び科学振興 52,743 (6.4)

KEYWORDS

キャッシュフロー
cash flow

企業活動に当てる現金や預金。これらの流れを、営業（通常の営業活動におけるキャッシュフロー）・投資（投資への支出・回収）・財務（資金の過不足の調整、株主還元）の3側面で示すものが、財務諸表の「キャッシュフロー計算書」。
☞ 2日目

黒字倒産
bankruptcy with a profit

売掛金のように、商品の売上は計上しても、その時点では実際の代金が回収されていないなどにより、帳簿上は黒字でも運転資金が不足して企業が倒産してしまうケース。

せた長期債務は、2007年末の財務省予想で773兆円もあるというのに、だ。

マキ：すっごい額ですね！　それじゃあ、営業利益が黒字になったとしても、政府は膨大な利息の支払いを抱えたまってわけですよね。しかも、その利息が営業利益より大きければ、結局、経常利益や当期純利益は赤字になってしまいますよね。

小浜：でも、もっと大事なのは、キャッシュフローのことなんだ。

マキ：「キャッシュフロー計算書」とかで出てきたキャッシュフローですか？

小浜：そう。キャッシュフローは、お金の流れ、あるいはお金の収支のことだと思えばいい。営業黒字であっても、融資の返済や利払いといった借金を返すための資金がなければ企業は倒産してしまう。つまり、キャッシュフローがなかったら、企業は倒産するんだ。

マキ：あ、それがいわゆる「黒字倒産」でしたっけ？

小浜：ああ。売上高や利益と比べて膨大な借金を抱えている企業の場合は、営業黒字であっても倒産する可能性がかなりあるんだよ。

マキ：つまり、営業黒字を達成するだけでは不十分で、抱えている借金を、いつまでに、どれだけ減らすかもちゃんと考えなければいけないんですね。

小浜：そういうこと！　でも問題はまだあるんだ。

Words & Phrases ①②③……は、その語が登場した行数を表しています。

- ② solve　（謎などを）解く、解決する
- ⑥ paper　新聞
- ⑩ tax revenues　税収、歳入
- ⑯ in the black　黒字で、利益があって
- ⑲ be relieved　ホッとする、安心する
- ⑳ expression　（特定の）言い回し、表現
- ㉔ neglect　無視する、放置する、顧みない
- ㉙ forecast　予想、予測、見通し
- ㉛ enormous　膨大な、非常に大きい
- ㉝ in the red　赤字（の状態）で
- ㊴ service　（負債を）返済する、償還する
- ㊻ achieve　獲得する、得る

Chapter 2

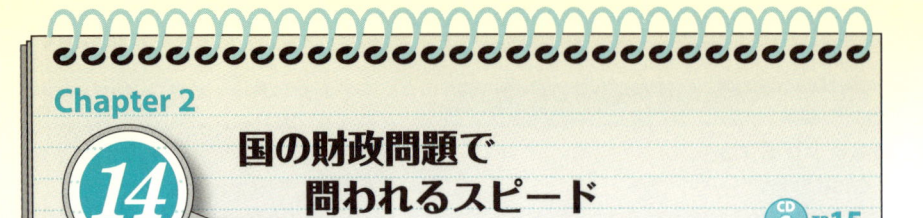

14日目 国の財政問題で問われるスピード

Prof. Obama: Let's continue our discussion on the primary balance issue. In 2006, the Japanese government announced, "The primary balance shall be even in 2011." In other words, the government said it would take more than five years to achieve an operating profit.

Maki: Really, five years? If it were a company, it would have gone bankrupt a long time ago. Is it really all right to take that long?

Obama: Yes, that's the second problem. If it were a company, the management would have to achieve an operating profit in about three years, even if the liabilities were small. Otherwise, banks would stop doing business with them. It's quite likely that the company would go bankrupt.

Maki: But, when Carlos Ghosn became president of Nissan Motor Company, he hurried to achieve an operating profit by cutting various expenses. He was called "Mr. Cost-Cutter", but he made the correct managerial judgment. Compared with him, the Japanese government is going far too slowly.

Obama: Yes, it is. To have an even primary balance in 2011 means that the operating loss will continue until 2010. Until then, the government loans will keep piling up.

Maki: But how much in loans is the government allowed to have?

Obama: Well, that's a difficult question to answer. As a reference, the EU's index for a healthy economy, and the initial condition for a government joining the EU, is: "The annual fiscal deficit is within 3% of the GDP, and the accumulated fiscal

KEYWORDS

EUの指標
EU's index
ここでは、EUが加盟国に対して達成することを求めている諸基準を指す。健全な経済状態を示す指標としては、財政赤字の上限のほか、為替相場の変動幅も設定されている。

GDP（国内総生産）
gross domestic product
国内で一定期間（通常は1年）に生み出される付加価値の合計。各企業の売上高から仕入れを引いた金額の総計で、マクロ経済における重要な指標。

TRANSLATION

小浜教授：さて、プライマリーバランスの問題について話を続けよう。「2011年にプライマリーバランスを均衡させる」と日本政府が発表したのは2006年。つまり政府は、営業黒字を達成するのに5年以上もかかると言ったんだ。

マキ：ええっ、5年も？ 企業だったらとっくに倒産していますね。そんなに時間がかかって、大丈夫なんですか？

小浜：そう、そこが2つ目の問題だ。企業だったら、たとえ借入れが少なくても、3年程度で営業黒字を達成させなければ駄目だろう。そうでなければ、銀行が取引を停止しかねなくて、その企業は倒産の危険性が高くなるからね。

マキ：でも、確かに日産も、カルロス・ゴーンさんが経営トップになった際、とにかく経費を削減して営業利益の黒字化を急ぎましたよね。ゴーンさんは「Mr.コストカッター」なんて言われましたけど、それは経営的には正しい判断だったんだ。それに比べて、日本政府ってすごくのんびりしているんですね。

小浜：そうなんだ。2011年にプライマリーバランスの収支が合うということは、2010年までは営業赤字が続くってこと。だからその間は、国の借金が増え続けることになる。

マキ：でも、政府はそもそも、どれくらい（の額）まで借金しても大丈夫なんですか？

小浜：うーん、難しい質問だ。参考までにEUへの当初の加盟条件を見ると、健全性の指標として、「毎年の財政赤字がGDPの3％以内、および財政赤字残高がGDPの60％まで」とされている。でも日本は、毎年の財政赤字がGDPの約5％、財政赤字残高はGDPの150％程度だ。

deficit is up to 60% of the GDP." Japan's annual fiscal deficit is about 5% of the GDP, and the accumulated fiscal deficit is 150% of the GDP.

Maki: Then, Japan wouldn't qualify to join the EU! It seems to me that the Japanese fiscal account is much worse than people realize. But why do we compare the fiscal deficit with the GDP? Don't we usually compare it with the income?

Obama: Good point! Do you know what the GDP is?

Maki: It's short for gross domestic product. It's the total amount of goods and services produced in a year within a country.

Obama: Yes, it means the "added value" in a certain period of time within a country. Most of it comes from the sales made by companies, while labor costs are paid with the money from the sales. If the GDP, which is the total of added value, does not increase, salary payments cannot be expected to grow.

Maki: Income tax is paid out of salaries, and the government uses that tax revenue to repay the loan. In this sense, I think it's meaningful to compare the ratio of the fiscal deficit to the GDP.

Obama: Yes, it is, because after all, the government's repayment ability depends on tax revenues. Just for your info, in fiscal year 2007, government expenditures were about 83 trillion yen, while the tax revenue was a little over 57 trillion yen. A little over 25 trillion yen of that deficit is covered by a loan called a "deficit-financing bond". In this way, the fiscal deficit expands every year.

Maki: Prof. Obama, I cannot understand at all why the government is so relaxed about all this.

KEYWORDS

付加価値
added value

企業の売上高から仕入れを引いたもの。人件費は、この付加価値から支払われる。付加価値に占める人件費の割合「労働分配率」は、マクロ経済にとっても企業経営にとっても重要な指標。

赤字国債
deficit-financing bond

国の一般会計予算のうち、経常経費の歳入不足を補うために発行する国債。発行には特別立法が必要で、公共工事などの財源となる建設国債とは区別される。

マキ：それじゃ、日本はEUに入れないじゃないですか！　日本の財政は、私たちが思っているよりうんと危ないみたいですね。でも、どうして財政赤字の規模をGDPと比べるんですか？　普通だったら収入と比較しませんか？

小浜：いいところに気付いたね。じゃあ、GDPってそもそも何だっけ？

マキ：gross domestic product、国内総生産の略称です。意味は、国内で1年間に生み出される財とサービスの価値の合計、ですよね。

小浜：そう、一定の期間に国内で生み出された「付加価値」のことだ。付加価値は、その多くを企業の売上高が占めていて、そこから人件費が払われている。そして、付加価値の総計であるGDPが伸びなければ、給料の支払いも伸びも期待できない。

マキ：そして、給料から所得税が納められて、その税収で政府は借金を返していくと。そう考えると、財政赤字の対GDP比率を見比べることも、ちょっとは納得できますね。

小浜：結局のところ、政府の返済能力は、税収などの収入によって決まるんだ。ちなみに平成19年度（2007年度）は、約83兆円の歳出に対して、税収は57兆円強。25兆円強の不足分は赤字国債という借金で賄われる。この調子で、財政赤字は毎年、膨らんでいくんだ。

マキ：もー、先生、政府がどうしてこんなにのんびりしているのか、私には全く理解できません。

Words & Phrases　①②③……は、その語が登場した行数を表しています。

- ③ in other words　言い換えれば
- ⑭ president　社長、代表取締役
- ⑰ managerial　経営（上）の
- ㉑ pile up　山積する、たまる
- ㉓ as a reference　参考として、参照用に
- ㉔ initial　最初の
- ㉖ accumulated　累積した
- ㉚ qualify to　〜する資格を得る
- ㊸ repay　（お金を）払い戻す、返済する
- ㊹ meaningful　意味のある、重要な
- ㊻ depends on　〜によって決まる

Chapter 2

15日目 日本政府が破綻しない理由

Maki: I know that Japan's fiscal deficit is really enormous, but how can we repay this loan? Is it really all right to keep increasing it?

Prof. Obama: That's a difficult question. In the case of a company, if the "net loan", which is the amount after deducting cash on hand and in banks from the loan amount, exceeds the annual added value of the company, the cash flow of the company often becomes tight.

Maki: You mean that the annual added value should be used for the repayment of the loan?

Obama: No, you cannot use the entire added value for the repayment of the loan. The salaries and other expenses must be paid, too. If a company can leave 10% of the added value as their profit, it is a fairly good company. The remaining amount after paying the tax from the profit is the money that can be used freely, which is called "free cash flow". In short, even in the case of a company making a healthy profit, the money that can be used for the loan repayment is only about 10 to 20% of the added value. An ordinary company cannot possibly use 30% for repayment.

Maki: Really? Only a small amount can be used for repayment! Then, how can we expect to return this huge 800 trillion yen loan?

Obama: Well. It's not so simple. Using the EU membership standard of the fiscal deficit being less than 60% of the GDP, a "healthy loan" amount would be about 300 trillion yen. Then, the Japanese government would have to return …

損益計算書

KEYWORDS

財政赤字
fiscal deficit
☞ 9日目、13日目

付加価値
added value
☞ 14日目

付加価値の何パーセントを返済に充てられるか

sales － purchase ＝ **added value**
売上高　　仕入れ　　　付加価値

- personnel expense　人件費
- cost of others　その他費用（仕入れ以外）
- tax　税
- profit　利益　← 付加価値の1割で十分
- repayment of debt　借入金返済

↓

借入期間で毎年の返済額が大きく変わる

TRANSLATION

マキ：日本の財政赤字がすごく大きいことは分かりました。でも結局のところ、どうしたらこの借金を返済できるんですか？ 借金がもっと増えても本当に大丈夫なんですか？

小浜教授：難しい質問だね。企業の場合だと、借入から現預金を引いた「ネット（純額）の借入」がその企業の年間の付加価値額を超えると、資金繰りが苦しくなる場合が多い。

マキ：借金の返済には、年間の付加価値額を充てるってことですか？

小浜：いや、付加価値額の全額を借入れの返済に充てることはできないんだ。給料やその他の経費も支払わなければならないからね。付加価値の1割を利益として残せれば、かなりいい会社と言えるだろう。利益として残った付加価値から税金を払った残りが、自由に使えるお金、フリーキャッシュフローということになる。要するに、利益が結構出ている会社でも、借金の返済に回せる資金は付加価値の1～2割程度で、3割を返済に回すのは、通常の会社だと難しいだろうね。

マキ：えー、返済に使えるのがそんなに少しだなんて！ これじゃ、800兆円なんて大きな借金を返済することは期待できないじゃないですか？

小浜：そう簡単にはいかないだろうね。EUの加盟条件である対GDP比60％以下を基準にすると、「健全な借金」の額は約300兆円。すると、日本政府が返済しなければならない借金は……

マキ：今すぐ500兆円だなんて！

小浜：この借金を税収で返済していくことになるんだけど、日本の1年間の税

● Chapter 2　15日目

Maki: Five hundred trillion yen right now!

Obama: We have to return this loan using tax revenue. Japan's tax revenue is about 50 trillion yen. So, it is about 10 years' tax revenue when simply calculated.

Maki: But in recent years, the annual expenditure has been about 80 trillion yen, which far exceeds tax revenue. That means that we cannot use tax revenue for the repayment! Isn't there a possibility that the Japanese government will go bankrupt?

Obama: There are two reasons why the Japanese government doesn't go bankrupt with this large amount of loans.

Maki: Two reasons?

Obama: Yes. As long as government credit is maintained, it can continue refinancing the loans. When the maturity date of the government bond comes, the government issues a refinancing bond and extends the repayment period. But, even in the case of refinancing, the government continues issuing new bonds for that amount as long as the financial deficit continues, so the accumulated financial deficit keeps on increasing.

Maki: That's no good! What's the other reason?

Obama: The other reason is that the government can adjust the length of the repayment period. At the time of refinancing, a 5-year bond may be extended to a 10-year bond; if extended to 20 years or 30 years, the annual repayment amount can be reduced.

Maki: But, that is just passing on the bill to later generations? In other words, our burden will increase. Oh, the Japanese government is in deep trouble with the economy!

KEYWORDS

償還期日
maturity date

金銭債務をその日までに弁済すべき期限・期日。金銭債務には、借入のほか、国債や社債などの債券も含まれる。支払い期日という意味ではdue dateも一般的に用いられる。

借換え債
refinancing bond

借り換えのために発行する国債のこと。政府は、大規模な建築物を造る費用を賄う際などに国債を発行するが、発行される国債の満期は、その建築物の耐用年数に合わせるのが原則。ただ、50年、60年といった長期の国債は市場で消化できないため、5年や10年といった短期国債を発行して、償還（返済）しては新たにまた短期国債の発行を繰り返す。これを借換え債と呼ぶ。

収は約50兆円だから、単純計算で約10年分の税収ということになるね。

マキ：でも、最近では、毎年の歳出が約80兆円にも達していて、これは税収を上回っていますよね。ということは、税収からも返済のしようがないってことじゃないですか！　日本政府が破綻してしまう可能性はないんですか？

小浜：これだけの借金を抱えていながら、日本政府がどうして破綻しないでいられるのか――それには2つ理由がある。

マキ：2つの理由？

小浜：そう。1つは政府の信用が維持される限り、借り換えが可能だということさ。つまり、国債の**償還期日**が来たら、**借換え債**を発行して、返済期間を先延ばしするんだ。もっとも、借り換えをしても、財政赤字が続く限りはその分だけ新しい国債を出し続けるわけだから、赤字残高は増え続ける。

マキ：ダメじゃないですか！　それで、もうひとつの理由は？

小浜：もうひとつの理由は、返済期間の調整を行えること。借り換えをするときに、5年国債を10年ものに、それをさらに20年、30年に延ばせば、毎年の返済負担を減らすことができるからね。

マキ：でもそれじゃ、ツケを後世に回しているだけですよ。つまり私たちの負担がまた増える。もう、日本政府の経営は、めちゃくちゃ問題だらけですね！

Words & Phrases

①②③……は、その語が登場した行数を表しています。

① enormous　巨大な、膨大な
⑥ exceed　上回る、超える
⑧ tight　（予算などが）逼迫した、厳しい
⑪ entire　すべての
⑭ fairly　かなり、相当に
⑭ remaining　残っている
⑯ in short　要するに、手短に言えば
⑯ in the case of　～の場合は、～については
㉒ expect　期待する、予期する
㉒ trillion　（1）兆
㊳ credit　信用（度）
㊴ refinance　借り換える、資金を補充する
(51) bill　請求書、ツケ
(51) generation　世代（の人々）
(52) burden　負担、重荷
(53) in deep trouble　非常に困った状態で、大きな問題になって

Chapter 2

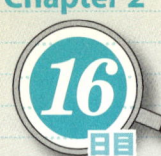

REVIEW EXERCISE

16日目

Chapter 2 で学んだ内容を復習しよう

CD1 TR17 まずは、チャンツのリズムに乗せて Keywords を発音しましょう。

- ☐ **fiscal deficit**
  財政赤字
- ☐ **net sales**
  売上高
- ☐ **assets turnover ratio**
  資産回転率
- ☐ **fiscal year**
  年度

- ☐ **gross profit**
  売上総利益
- ☐ **cost of sales**
  売上原価
- ☐ **cost of production**
  製造原価
- ☐ **inventory**
  棚卸資産

< pause >

- ☐ **dead stock**
  不良在庫
- ☐ **cost of sales ratio**
  売上原価率
- ☐ **operating profit**
  営業利益
- ☐ **ordinary profit**
  経常利益

- ☐ **net profit**
  当期純利益
- ☐ **general administrative expenses**
  一般管理費
- ☐ **profit and loss**
  損益
- ☐ **special gains**
  特別利益

< pause >

- ☐ **special losses**
  特別損失
- ☐ **primary balance**
  プライマリーバランス
- ☐ **repayment**
  元金払い
- ☐ **cash flow**
  キャッシュフロー

- ☐ **bankruptcy**
  倒産
- ☐ **index**
  指標
- ☐ **gross domestic product**
  国内総生産
- ☐ **added value**
  付加価値

< pause >

- ☐ **deficit-financing bond**
  赤字国債
- ☐ **maturity date**
  償還期日
- ☐ **refinancing bond**
  借換え債
- ☐ **shrink**
  縮まる、小さくなる

- ☐ **personnel expense**
  人件費
- ☐ **fluctuation**
  変動、ばらつき
- ☐ **book value**
  帳簿価格
- ☐ **tax revenues**
  税収、歳入

会社の実力を英語で診断！

損益計算書と、必要な場合は貸借対照表（43ページ）も見ながら、以下の問いに答えましょう。

A社　Statement of Income

Net sales		26,000
Cost of sales *1		21,000
(　　　　profit)		5,000
Selling and general administrative expenses *2		2,500
(　　　　profit)		2,500
Non-operating income		
Interest and dividend income	100	
Other non-operating income	100	200
Non-operating expenses		
Interest expense	150	150
(　　　　profit)		2,550
Extraordinary gains		60
Extraordinary losses	10	50
(　　　　profit before income taxes)		2,600
Income taxes - current		900
Income taxes - deferred	100	1,000
(　　　　profit)		1,600

B社　Statement of Income

Net sales		24,000
Cost of sales *1		19,500
(　　　　profit)		4,500
Selling and general administrative expenses *2		4,000
(　　　　profit)		500
Non-operating income		
Interest and dividend income	50	
Other non-operating income	30	80
Non-operating expenses		
Interest expense	240	240
(　　　　profit)		340
Extraordinary gains		360
Extraordinary losses	200	160
(　　　　profit before income taxes)		180
Income taxes - current		70
Income taxes - deferred	0	70
(　　　　profit)		110

A社
*1 Schedule of Cost of sales
Purchase of raw material　7,000
Labor cost　9,000
Outsoucing cost　3,000
Depreciation　700
Utilities　1,300

*2 Schedule of Selling and general administrative expenses
Personnel expenses　1,300
Utilities　100
Rent　500
Advertising　300
Depreciation　100
Telephone and postage　200

B社
*1 Schedule of Cost of sales
Purchase of raw material　6,700
Labor cost　9,000
Outsoucing cost　2,000
Depreciation　500
Utilities　1,300

*2 Schedule of Selling and general administrative expenses
Personnel expenses　2,700
Utilities　100
Rent　500
Advertising　400
Depreciation　100
Telephone and postage　200

問1 損益計算書を見るときは、売上高の増減をチェックすることが重要です。その際、貸借対照表も併せて分析すると有用な数値があります。その計算式を英語と日本語で示し、A、B両社について、その数値を計算してください。
　＊A社、B社の貸借対照表は、Chapter 1 の Review Exercise（p.43）にあります。
　計算式　英（　　　　）＝（　　　　）／（　　　　）A社：
　　　　　日（　　　　）＝（　　　　）／（　　　　）B社：

問2 増収増益でありながら、売上の伸びほどには「売上総利益」や「営業利益」が増えないことがあります。それぞれ、財務諸表のどの数値を見ることで分かりますか。計算式を英語と日本語で示して、両社について試算してください。
　売上総利益　英（　　　　）＝（　　　　）／（　　　　）A社：
　　　　　　　日（　　　　）＝（　　　　）／（　　　　）B社：
　営業利益　　英（　　　　）＝（　　　　）／（　　　　）A社：
　　　　　　　日（　　　　）＝（　　　　）／（　　　　）B社：

問3 A、B2社の損益計算書の各利益の欄に、正しい名称を書き込み、日本語に訳してください。

解答と解説

A社　損益計算書

売上高		26,000
売上原価（注1）		21,000
（売上総利益）		5,000
販売費及び一般管理費(注2)		2,500
（営業利益）		2,500
営業外収益		
受取利息及び配当金	100	
その他	100	200
営業外費用		
支払利息	150	150
（経常利益）		2,550
特別利益	60	
特別損失	10	50
（税金等調整前当期純利益）		2,600
法人税、住民税及び事業税	900	
法人税等調整額	100	1,000
（当期純利益）		1,600

B社　損益計算書

売上高		24,000
売上原価（注1）		19,500
（売上総利益）		4,500
販売費及び一般管理費(注2)		4,000
（営業利益）		500
営業外収益		
受取利息及び配当金	50	
その他	30	80
営業外費用		
支払利息	240	240
（経常利益）		340
特別利益	360	
特別損失	200	160
（税金等調整前当期純利益）		180
法人税、住民税及び事業税	70	
法人税等調整額	0	70
（当期純利益）		110

（注1）売上原価の内訳
材料仕入	7,000
人件費	9,000
外注費	3,000
減価償却費	700
光熱費	1,300

（注2）販売費及び一般管理費の内訳
人件費	1,300
光熱費	100
賃借料	500
広告宣伝費	300
減価償却費	100
通信運搬費	200

（注1）売上原価の内訳
材料仕入	6,700
人件費	9,000
外注費	2,000
減価償却費	500
光熱費	1,300

（注2）販売費及び一般管理費の内訳
人件費	2,700
光熱費	100
賃借料	500
広告宣伝費	400
減価償却費	100
通信運搬費	200

問1　計算式　英 assets turnover ratio = net sales ／ total assets
　　　　　　　日（資産回転率）＝（売上高）／（資産）
　　　　　　　A社：26,000 ÷ 32,000 = 0.81 回
　　　　　　　B社：24,000 ÷ 32,000 = 0.75 回

問2　売上総利益　英 cost of sale ratio = cost of sales ／ net sales
　　　　　　　　　　日（売上原価率）＝（売上原価）／（売上高）
　　　　　　　　　　A社：21,000 ÷ 26,000 = 80.8%
　　　　　　　　　　B社：19,500 ÷ 24,000 = 81.3%
　　　　営業利益　　英 selling and general administrative expenses
　　　　　　　　　　日（販管費率）＝（販管費）／（売上高）
　　　　　　　　　　A社：2,500 ÷ 26,000 = 9.6%
　　　　　　　　　　B社：4,000 ÷ 24,000 = 16.7%

問3　上から、英語では Gross、Operating、Ordinary、Net、Net。日本語では、売上総（利益）、営業（利益）、経常（利益）、当期純（利益）。詳細は、日本語版の損益計算書内の各利益欄を参照。

【解説】 表内では米式に「利益」を「profit」と記載しているが、Chapter 2 で言われているように income を用いてもよい。

Chapter 2 のまとめ

●損益計算書（Profit Loss Statement: P/L）とは……

ある一定期間の売上高から経費を順に引いていき、当期利益（最終的にその期にいくら儲かったかを示す数字）を表示するものです

		科目	金額
経常損益	営業損益 operating profit and loss	売上高 net sales	
		売上原価 cost of sales	
		売上総利益 gross profit	
		販管費 selling and general administrative expenses	
		営業利益 operating profit	
	営業外損益 non-operating profit and loss	営業外収益	
		営業外費用	
	経常利益 ordinary profit		
特別損益 special gains and losses	特別利益 special losses		
	特別損失 special gains		
税引前当期利益			
法人税等			
当期利益 net income			

●下線部に対応する英語を記入しながら、学習内容を最後にまとめましょう。

損益計算書の注目点！

売上高は、前期と比べて「増減」を見る

損益計算書は、貸借対照表と併せてチェックする！

資産の増減率と売上高の増減率では、売上高の伸び率が大きいのが正常

資産と売上高の関係、すなわち資産回転率（売上高／資産）は高いか？

政府のプライマリーバランスは営業利益に相当すると考える

Column 2

自己資本比率の計算式と自己資本と株主資本

　単純化すると、自己資本比率は「純資産÷資産」です。しかし、正確には、純資産の中から少数株主持分を引いたものを「自己資本」とし、「自己資本÷資産」と計算することもあります。もっとも、少数株主持分が多くの会社ではそれほど多くないことや、返済義務がない資金であることを考えれば、「純資産÷資産」でもOKです。

　ちなみに、私は「自己資本」という言い方があまり好きではありません。いかにも「資本（純資産）は会社のもの」というような言い方だからです。事実、従来は自己資本を経営者が自分のものとして扱うがごとき経営が普通に行われていました。しかし、資本は紛れもなく株主のものです。そして株主は、負債とは異なるリスクを引き受けて、資金を会社に提供しているのです。よって資本は、自己資本ではなく株主資本と呼ぶのが適当です。

　なお、2006年の会社法施行により、従来の「資本」が、「純資産」という名称に変わりました。細かい話ですが、その純資産の中で、資本金、資本剰余金、利益剰余金などを「株主資本」、それに有価証券の評価損益のような「評価・換算差額等」を加えたものを「自己資本」、さらに、それに少数株主持分を加えたものが「純資産」と呼ばれるようになりました。（こ）

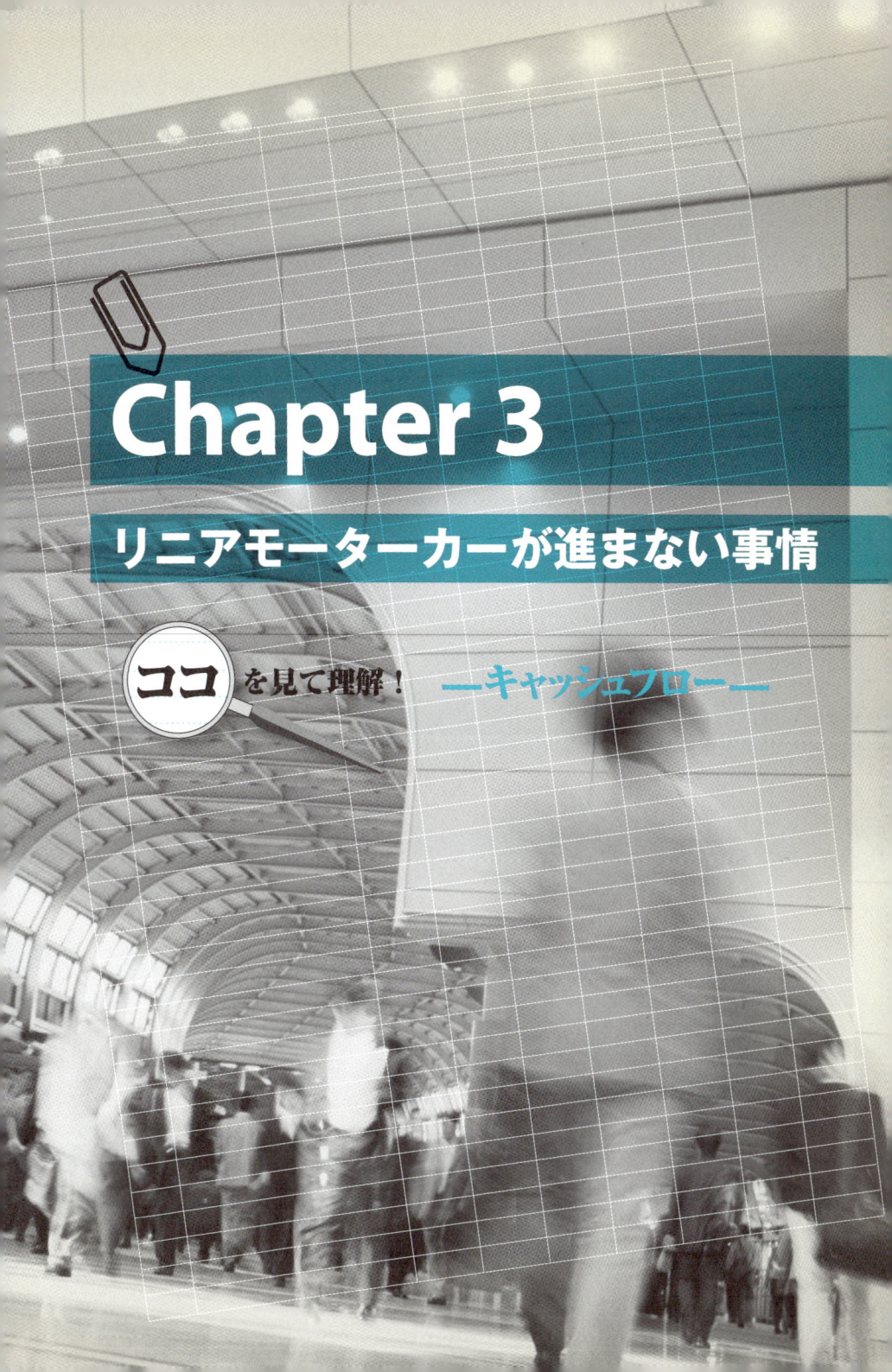

Chapter 3

リニアモーターカーが進まない事情

ココを見て理解！　――キャッシュフロー――

Chapter 3

17日目 キャッシュフロー計算書と営業キャッシュフロー

TR18

Maki: Hello, Professor Obama! I went to Tokyo last weekend to see a friend. I usually go to Tokyo by night bus, but I went by *shinkansen* this time, and I was surprised. It was so quick to reach Tokyo. I'm thinking of using the *shinkansen* every time from now on.

Prof. Obama: It's more expensive to go by *shinkansen*, but it does save time. I hear that the Linear Express will take you from Tokyo to Nagoya in less than one hour. Tokyo will seem much closer then.

Maki: I read about it in the newspaper. I want it to be completed soon, but the construction hasn't even started. Then there's the Second Tomei Expressway —its construction was started a long time ago, but there's almost no progress. Why is the government so slow in proceeding with public works? It's really strange.

Obama: There are various reasons for the snail's pace. One of the reasons is the government's cash flow problem.

Maki: I often hear the term "cash flow". Professors use it in class, "Cash flow statements are very important". Are they that important?

Obama: Yes, a cash flow statement is quite important. It's one of the "three financial statements", together with the balance sheet and the income statement. Let's review what "cash flow" is.

Maki: It's what you talked about regarding "cash-in and cash-out" last time, isn't it? Isn't it the money earned by the company, and the same as profit?

KEYWORDS

リニア新幹線
Linear Express
時速 500km で走行する超電導磁気浮上式リニアモーターカーによって、東京都から甲府市、名古屋市、奈良市付近を経過して終点の大阪市までを、約1時間で結ぼうとするもの。一般にリニアモーターカーとは、磁気浮上式と鉄輪式に分かれるが、高速性や近未来性から前者のみをリニアモーターカーと呼ぶことがある。

第二東名
Second Tomei Expressway
現在建設中の新東名高速道路の通称。神奈川県海老名市から静岡県を経由し愛知県豊田市へ至る予定だが、一部は未着工で、海老名南 JCT 以東のルートや事業化は未定。

財務三表
three financial statements
2000 年 3 月期（1999 年度末）から決算制度が変更され、連結決算制度が始まった際に導入されたキャッシュフロー計算書と、従来からあった貸借対照表と損益計算書を合わせた 3 つの財務諸表の呼称。ちなみに、2000 年 3 月期まで必要とされていたのは、貸借対照表と損益計算書の 2 つで、「財務二表」と呼ばれていた。
☞ 2 日目、9 日目

現金の出入り（収支）
cash-in and cash-out
会計帳簿の記帳方法には「現金主義」と「発生主義」がある。現金の出入りを伴う取引の場合、いずれの方法を採用するかによって、帳簿記帳の時期が異なる。

TRANSLATION

マキ：小浜先生、こんにちは。先週末に、友達に会いに東京へ行ってきたんですよ。いつもは夜行バスで行くんですけど、今回初めて新幹線を使ったら、あっという間に東京に着いてビックリ！これからはいつも新幹線にしようかなと思って。

小浜教授：新幹線で行く方が高いけど、確かに時間の節約になるからね。でも、リニアができたら、東京 – 名古屋間は 1 時間を切るらしいぞ。東京がますます近くなるね。

マキ：それ、新聞で読みました！　早く完成してほしいのに、着工すらしてないんですよね。そういえば第二東名も、ずっと前から工事しているのに、全然はかどらないし。公共事業って、どうしてあんなに遅いんですか？　本当に不思議です。

小浜：あの遅さにはいろいろな原因があるんだけど、ひとつには、政府のキャッシュフローの問題がある。

マキ：この間から、「キャッシュフロー」って言葉がよく出てきますね。授業でも、先生方が「キャッシュフロー計算書は大事だ」と言っているのをよく聞きますけど、そんなに大切なんですか？

小浜：そうさ。キャッシュフロー計算書はすごく大切で、貸借対照表、損益計算書と合わせて「財務三表」と呼ばれるものの 1 つなんだ。じゃあ、「キャッシュフロー」って何のことか、おさらいしておこうか？

マキ：先生がこの前、「現金の出入り（収支）のこと」っておっしゃっていたもののことですよね。ってことは、企業が稼いだお金、つまり利益のことじゃないですか？

Obama: Not quite. That's a typical misunderstanding. Cash flow is the inflow and outflow of cash, so it's quite different from profit. Even if there's a profit, the cash flow may be negative, and vice versa.

Maki: How can that be?

Obama: Well, one reason is that there are expenses without cash-outs.

Maki: Expenses without cash-outs? What do you mean?

Obama: The valuation loss of securities is one example. If the value of the company's securities goes down, the valuation loss is calculated and the profit is adjusted down accordingly. As you can see, no cash has gone in or out, so it is irrelevant to cash flow.

Maki: Oh, I see!

キャッシュフロー

KEYWORDS

評価損
valuation loss

例えば、企業が所有している有価証券の価値が下がった場合などに生じる損失。評価損は、損益計算書に費用として計上される。英語ではappraisal lossesと呼ばれることもある。

小浜：いやあ、残念。それは典型的な勘違い。キャッシュフローとは現金の出入りそのもののことであって、損益とは違うんだ。利益が出ていてもキャッシュフローがマイナスなこともあれば、その逆もあるからね。

マキ：どうしてそんなことがあり得るんですか？

小浜：ひとつには、現金の支出を伴わない費用があるからだ。

マキ：現金が出ていかない費用？ どういうことですか？

小浜：例えば、有価証券の評価損。企業が所有している証券の価値が下がると、損益計算書では費用として評価損が算定され、それに応じて利益が減る。だけど分かるように、お金自体は、出ていっても入ってきてもいないから、キャッシュフローには関係ない。

マキ：あ、なるほど！

Words & Phrases　①②③……は、その語が登場した行数を表しています。

- ④ think of　〜と考える、〜について考える
- ⑦ save　節約する
- ⑫ construction　建設、建造、建築
- ⑭ proceed with　〜を進める、始める
- ⑭ public works　公共工事
- ㉓ review　復習する
- ㉕ earn　稼ぐ、得る
- ㉙ negative　マイナスの
- ㉙ vice versa　逆もまた同様
- ㉜ expense　費用、経費、支出
- ㊱ securities　有価証券、債権
- ㊲ calculate　算出する
- ㊲ accordingly　〜に応じて
- ㊳ irrelevant　関係がない⇔relevant

Chapter 3

18日目 お金が出て行かない費用とは？

Maki: There are expenses that do not cause cash to go out, and similarly some securities might rise in value without any cash coming in. So, depending on the increase and decrease of such expenses, the profit on the books fluctuates. On the other hand, cash flow is the money that actually moves regardless of the increase and decrease of the profit. So that means that in the case of goods sold that haven't been paid for, or in the case of the goods bought that haven't been paid for yet, there will be a difference between the profit and the cash flow.

Prof. Obama: Yes, you've hit the nail on the head. Money that hasn't been received is called "accounts receivable", and money that hasn't been paid is called "accounts payable". These are directly connected to cash flow. It's the same with "depreciation". When a company invests in equipment, the money goes out at that time as cash flow. But, later on, "depreciation" is calculated for each period of the equipment's use, and this is shown as an expense without a cash-out.

Maki: I see. So, even if there is a profit on the books, cash may not come in, or there may be a loss where money does not go out.

Obama: Right. And there are three sections in a cash flow statement. "Cash flow from operating activities" shows how much cash flow a company earned or lost through ordinary operating activities. Very roughly speaking, it is calculated by subtracting "expenses without cash expenditures" from "net profit". So, it's important for a company to earn "cash flow from operating activities".

KEYWORDS

売掛金
accounts receivable
製品やサービスを売ったけれども、代金を回収していない状態。

買掛金
accounts payable
製品やサービスを買ったけれども、代金を支払っていない状態。

（有形固定資産の）減価償却費
depreciation
設備投資のうち、工場や機械など耐用年数に限りのあるものについて、毎年減額されていく資産価値を費用化して示したもの。その期間の設備や機械の価値の目減り分。無形固定資産の償却は amortization という。

営業キャッシュフロー
cash flow from operating activities
売掛金・買掛金・在庫といった営業循環上の資金の動きや、所有している有価証券などに生じる評価損や減価償却費などの、現金の支出を伴わない費用について資金の動きを示すもの。

現金の支出を伴わない費用
expenses without cash expenditures
所有している有価証券などに生じる評価損や減価償却費など。営業キャッシュフローの一部を構成する。

TRANSLATION

マキ：お金の出ていかない費用が存在するけど、同様に、お金が入ってこないのに価値が上がる有価証券がある。だから、そうした費用の増減次第で、帳簿上の利益が変動する。一方で、利益の増減とは関係なく、実際に動いているお金がキャッシュフロー。つまり、商品を売ったのにまだ代金を回収していない場合とか、買ったけれどお金を支払っていない場合とかも、利益とキャッシュフローに違いが生じるってことですよね。

小浜教授：そう、うまく的を射たね。回収されていない代金を売掛金、残っている支払額を買掛金と呼ぶんだけど、これらはキャッシュフローに直結している。あとは、減価償却費も同様だ。企業が設備などに投資すると、その時にお金が出ていってキャッシュフローが発生する。だけど、減価償却費という費用は設備の使用期間に応じて後から計上されるから、それがお金の出て行かない費用になる。

マキ：なるほど。帳簿上で利益があってもキャッシュが入ってこないことや、お金が出て行かなくても損をしていることがあるんですね。

小浜：そうさ。キャッシュフロー計算書には3つのセクションがあって、通常の営業活動で企業がどれだけのキャッシュフローを得たか、あるいは失ったのかを表すのが「営業キャッシュフロー」で、ごくごく大ざっぱに言うと、「純利益」から「現金の支出を伴わない費用」を引いたものと言える。だから企業にとっては「営業キャッシュフロー」を稼ぐことが大切なんだ。

Maki: Yes, I see, because even if a company had an operating profit, it wouldn't have any cash left on hand if cash flow from operating activities was negative.

Obama: Exactly. A company goes bankrupt if cash flow from operating activities is negative. So, keeping cash flow from operating activities positive is very important.

Maki: Well, you've cleared that up for me: profit and cash flow are entirely different. I'll remember that!

日産自動車の連結キャッシュフロー計算書

（百万円未満四捨五入）

科目	平成 12 年 (12/4 ～ 13/3)	平成 11 年 (11/4 ～ 12/3)
	百万円	百万円
Ⅰ　営業活動によるキャッシュフロー		
税金等調整前当期純利益	289,698	△ 712,654
減価償却費	360,191	434,553
：		
計	73,251	292,091
Ⅱ　投資活動によるキャッシュフロー		
：		
有形固定資産の取得による収入	△ 197,216	△ 238,347
有形固定資産の売却による収入	98,692	85,859
リース資産の増加額	△ 170,146	△ 153,793
：		
計	△ 15,585	△ 180,412

KEYWORDS

マキ：そうですね。たとえ営業利益が黒字でも、営業キャッシュフローがマイナスになってしまったら、手元には全然、現預金が残らないわけですから。

小浜：その通り。営業キャッシュフローがマイナスだと、企業は倒産してしまう。だから、営業キャッシュフローをプラスにしておくことは非常に大切なんだ。

マキ：なるほど、おかげでよく分かりました。利益とキャッシュフローはまったく別ものなんですね。覚えておきます！

Words & Phrases   ①②③……は、その語が登場した行数を表しています。

② similarly　同様に、同じく
④ books　帳簿、会計簿
④ fluctuate　変動する、上下する
⑤ regardless of　〜にかかわらず
⑩ hit the nail on the head　うまく言う、要点をつく
㉓ subtract　差し引く、控除する
㉘ on hand　手元に
㉞ entirely　完全に、全く

Chapter 3

19日目 投資キャッシュフローと未来投資

Maki: By the way, Professor Obama, after we talked about Nissan, I went and read a bit more about them. They made a V-shaped recovery from their management crisis, didn't they? From fiscal year 1999, when Carlos Ghosn became president, to fiscal year 2001, Nissan went from a 680 billion yen loss to a 370 billion yen profit. That's fantastic, isn't it?

Prof. Obama: Yes, it is. But, in the fiscal year ended March 2007, while Toyota and Honda increased both net sales and net profit, Nissan's profit didn't increase even though their sales did.

Maki: Really? So, their profits decreased? I thought Nissan was back on track after the V-shaped recovery. Maybe that's why we don't hear about Mr. Ghosn so much lately. As for new technology developments such as hybrid cars, we don't hear about Nissan there, either. What's happened?

Obama: That's a good point! If we look at Nissan's cash flow statements during its V-shaped recovery period, we can see signs of its likely decreased profit in the future. A cash flow statement is divided into three sections. Here, you see "cash flow from operating activities" which I've already explained. The remaining two sections are "cash flow from investing activities" and "cash flow from financing activities."

Maki: So, cash flow from investing activities shows the movement of the money used by a company for investment, and cash flow from financing activities shows the movement of the money used for financing activities such as money procurement. Is that right?

Keywords

V字回復
V-shaped recovery
企業の収益に関して、中長期的に下降線をたどっていたものが、急激に上昇基調に転じることを指す。ここで引用されているのは、1990年代後半に危機に陥った日産自動車のV字回復。

投資キャッシュフロー
cash flow from investing activities
企業が投資にどれだけの資金を費やしたか、その投資からどれだけの金額を回収したかを示す。投資キャッシュフローを見る際は「未来投資をしているかどうか」が最重要ポイントとなる。

財務キャッシュフロー
cash flow from financing activities
財務活動でのキャッシュフローの動きを示す。内訳は、借り入れ・社債・増資などでの資金調達や資金償還と、配当や自社株式買い入れなどの株主還元に大別される。

Translation

マキ：ところで先生、日産の例が出たので、自分で少し調べてみたんです。日産って、経営危機からV字回復したんですよね？ カルロス・ゴーンさんが経営者に就任した平成11年度（1999年度）から13年度（2001年度）の間に、6800億円の赤字から一転、3700億円の黒字へ転換したとか。すごいですね〜！

小浜教授：そうだね。でも、2007年3月期決算で、トヨタやホンダは増収増益なんだが、日産は、増収なのに減益になっているんだよ。

マキ：え？ 利益が減ったんですか？ V字回復してからは、日産も軌道に乗っているとばかり思っていました。でも、そのせいか、最近はゴーンさんの話もあまり聞かないですし、ハイブリッドカーとかの新しい技術開発のことでも、日産の名前はあまり出てきませんね。何があったんですか？

小浜：いいところに目を付けたね。日産の減益の予兆は、実は、V字回復をしていた時期のキャッシュフロー計算書を見れば、読み解くことができるんだ。前に、キャッシュフロー計算書は3つのセクションに分かれているって話したけど、ここで見るのはそのうちの「営業キャッシュフロー」で、これは前に説明したよね。で、残る2つは、「投資キャッシュフロー」と「財務キャッシュフロー」というんだ。

マキ：ええと、投資キャッシュフローは、企業が投資のために使ったお金の動きで、財務キャッシュフローは、資金調達みたいな財務活動のために使われたお金の動き、ってとこですか？

● Chapter 3 19日目

Obama: That's about right. From a different angle, we can say that cash flow from operating activities is "to earn", and cash flow from investing activities and cash flow from financing activities are "to spend". The point of looking at cash flow from investing activities is to see whether or not the company is spending money on "future investments".

Maki: Future investments?

Obama: Whether the company is investing money in its future or not; you can tell this by looking at whether "acquisition of tangible fixed assets" exceeds "depreciation" or not. As I said earlier, depreciation is the reduced value of the equipment and machinery during a certain period. If the company doesn't reinvest money in about an amount equal to depreciation, it won't even be able to maintain its current activities.

Maki: I see. If the company doesn't at least make up for the reduced value, the equipment becomes older and older, and the business gets smaller.

キャッシュフロー計算書の仕組み

cash flow from operating activities
〔営業キャッシュフロー〕…通常の営業活動でのキャッシュ
　　　　　　　　　　　　　フロー
　　　　　　　　　　　　→「稼ぐ」必要
　　　　　　　　　　　▶「稼ぐ」こと（＋）が原則

cash flow from investing activities
〔投資キャッシュフロー〕…投資への支出、回収
　　　　　　　　　　　　→未来投資、現事業維持投資
　　　　　　　　　　　　　財務投資、資産売却
　　　　　　　　　　　▶「使う」こと（−）が原則

cash flow from financing activities
〔財務キャッシュフロー〕…資金の過不足の調整、株主還元
　　　　　　　　　　　▶「使う」こと（−）が原則

KEYWORDS

未来投資
future investments

現事業を維持するだけでなく、それを発展させるために行う投資。財務諸表に表れる設備投資のほか、企業の将来を担うような人材への投資も含まれる。

有形固定資産の取得
acquisition of tangible fixed assets

有形固定資産を取得する際、帳簿に計上される取得原価は、購入代金のほか、手数料・改造費用・登記費用・取得費など購入に要した費用を含める。tangible fixed assets（有形固定資産）とは、企業が長期にわたって事業活動に利用する資産で、建物・設備・土地など、具体的に目に見える有体物を指す。

小浜：そんなところだ。違う見方をすると、営業キャッシュフローは「稼ぐ」ことで、投資キャッシュフローと財務キャッシュフローは「使う」ことと言える。それで、投資キャッシュフローを見るときのポイントは、「未来投資」をしているかどうか、という点なんだ。

マキ：未来投資？

小浜：そう。未来投資をしているかどうかは、「有形固定資産の取得」が「減価償却費」を上回っているかどうか、で見分けることができる。減価償却費というのは、前にも話したように、一定期間における設備や機械の価値の目減り分だ。だから減価償却費分くらいは再投資を行わないと、企業は、今取り組んでいる事業を維持することすら難しくなる、というわけだ。

マキ：なるほど。最低限、減った分だけでも補っていかないと、設備はどんどん古くなって事業が縮小しちゃいますもんね。

Words & Phrases   ①②③……は、その語が登場した行数を表しています。

⑪ back on track　再び軌道に乗って
⑫ lately　最近
⑬ hybrid car　ハイブリッド車、ガソリンと電気の両方を電力源とする車。hybridは「複合型の」
㉕ procurement　調達、入手
㊱ exceed　上回る、超える
㊲ equipment　設備、装置
㊳ machinery　機械（類）
㊶ make up for　補う、埋め合わせる

Chapter 3

20日目 日産のV字回復と未来投資

TR21

Maki: What was Nissan's investment like?

Prof. Obama: Well, let's look at their cash flow statement*. In both fiscal years 1999 and 2000, depreciation of fixed assets was about 400 billion yen. Meanwhile, expenditure due to the acquisition of tangible fixed assets was 238.3 billion yen in fiscal year 1999 and 197.2 billion yen in fiscal year 2000.

　On the other hand, "income due to the sale of fixed tangible assets" was a little less than 100 billion yen in each year. Even if we add the increased amount of leased assets, the net acquisition of fixed assets, or "acquisitions minus sales", shows a very big decrease. In other words, Nissan reduced its investments tremendously.

Maki: Oh, I see. So, they made a profit by giving priority to the reorganization of their business through the sale of assets and restructuring, but the reduction of investment in this period has affected their current business performance. Well, now I know about "cash flow from operating activities" and "cash flow from investing activities", but I'm still not sure about "cash flow from financing activities".

Obama: Cash flow from financing activities shows the movement of money "used" in the financial activities of a company. In more concrete terms, it is money a company procures by taking out loans and by issuing corporate bonds, and money a company returns to shareholders as dividends and purchase of their own stock. If cash flow from financing activities is positive, it means that the company has received money through loans

KEYWORDS

リース資産
leased assets
生産設備用の機械や輸送機械、情報通信機器など、企業が購入し、別の企業（利用者）に一定期間の契約で有料貸し出しされる物品。

社債
corporate bond
企業が資金調達を目的として、投資家からの金銭の払い込みと引き替えに発行（起債）する債券。狭義には、会社法の規定するものを指す。
☞ 6日目

配当
dividend
企業活動においては、株主が受け取ることができる利益の分配。一般には現金配当を指す。会社法では、株式・社債・新株予約権は除かれる。

TRANSLATION

マキ：日産の投資はどうなっていたんですか？

小浜教授：よし、じゃあ日産のキャッシュフロー計算書*を見てみよう。平成11年度（1999年度）と平成12年度（2000年度）はどちらも、固定資産の減価償却費が、約4000億円。

それに対して、有形固定資産の取得による支出は、平成11年度が2383億円、平成12年度が1972億円。一方で「有形固定資産の売却による収入」がそれぞれの年に約1000億円弱ずつあるから、リース資産の増加額を加えても、ネット、つまり「取得−売却」での固定資産上の取得は、大幅なマイナスになっていることが分かるね。つまり、この時期日産は、投資を大幅に抑えていたんだ。

マキ：ふーん。つまり、資産の売却やリストラなどを行って事業の再建を優先して、営業黒字を出せるようにはなったけれど、この時の投資の抑制が現在の業績にも影響しているってことですね。それで先生、「営業キャッシュフロー」と「投資キャッシュフロー」は理解できたんですけど、「財務キャッシュフロー」ってどんなものか、まだよく分からなくて。

小浜：財務キャッシュフローは、企業が財務活動で「使う」お金の流れを表している。具体的には、企業が借入や社債の発行などで調達する資金や、配当や自社株買入れなどで主に還元するキャッシュのことを言う。財務キャッシュフローが「プラス」であれば借入

＊日産自動車のキャッシュフロー計算書（平成12年度）は、90ページを参照。

and capital issuance. Conversely, if it is negative, it means that the company has paid money as returns to shareholders and loan repayments.

Maki: So, is it better that cash flow from financing activities is negative? If the company continues increasing cash by loans and capital issuance, that's bad, isn't it?

Obama: Well, they certainly need to procure money, but it is a problem if cash flow from financing activities is always positive. It should be negative in a stable period if it's a sound company.

Maki: Oh, right. You can really see a company from a different angle if you read its cash flow statement.

あるべき姿はコレ！

⊖ cash flow from investing activities
投資キャッシュフロー
cash flow from financing activities
財務キャッシュフロー

⊕ cash flow from operating activities
営業キャッシュフロー

Keywords

増資
capital issuance

「融資」が、金融機関からの借り入れを意味し、返済義務を伴うのに対して、「増資」での資金提供は、株式の issuance（発行）を通して行われるため、増資による資金は、返済義務のない自己資金になる。

や増資などでお金が入ってきたということで、逆に「マイナス」であれば、株主還元や借入返済でお金を支払った、ということだ。

マキ：ってことは、財務キャッシュフローはマイナスになっていた方がいいってことですね。いつも借入や増資をしてキャッシュを増やしているようじゃいけないですもん。

小浜：資金調達は確かに必要なんだが、財務キャッシュフローが常にプラスなのは問題で、健全な企業であれば、安定期にはマイナスであるべきなんだ。

マキ：なるほど。キャッシュフロー計算書を使えば、また別の視点から企業を見られるようになるんですね。

Words & Phrases

①②③……は、その語が登場した行数を表しています。

- ④ meanwhile　その一方で
- ④ expenditure　支払額、費用
- ④ due to　〜のための
- ④ acquisition　取得、獲得
- ⑫ tremendously　ものすごく、大いに
- ⑬ give priority　優先的に取り扱う
- ⑭ reorganization　再編成、改造、革新
- ⑯ affect　影響する
- ⑯ performance　成果、パフォーマンス
- ㉒ concrete　具体的な、明確な
- ㉔ purchase　購入、買い入れ
- ㉗ Conversely,　逆に言えば
- ㉙ repayments　返済、払い戻し
- ㉚ negative　マイナスの数字
- ㉞ positive　正の、プラスの
- ㉟ sound　健全な、正常な

Chapter 3

21日目 キャッシュフロー経営の基本は「稼ぐ」と「使う」

Prof. Obama: By the way, do you know about cash flow management?

Maki: No, I don't. But it sounds like management that emphasizes cash flow.

Obama: Right. The fundamentals of cash flow management are "to earn" and "to spend". What that means is that a company has to earn money through its "cash flow from operating activities," and it has to limit the amount it spends on "cash flow from investing activities" and "cash flow from financing activities" by making sure it isn't more than the amount it earns. That's all.

Maki: That sounds logical. If you spend more than you earn, you make a loss.

Obama: But, the important thing is how to spend money, particularly on "future investments", in order to aim at the future development of the company while maintaining the current business. Future investments include not only investments in plant and equipment but also investments in human resources, which may lead to the improvement of the company. In addition to future investments, "returns to the shareholders" are also important in maintaining the share price. A company with poor financial performance needs to give priority to "financial improvement" by spending the earned cash flow.

Maki: So, it's best if money that's invested comes from the earned cash flow from operating activities. The point of management is to earn as much as possible from cash flow from operating activities.

KEYWORDS

株主還元
returns to the shareholders
株価を維持するためには現在の株主への還元が不可欠。配当などの形で行われ、営業キャッシュフローから現事業維持のために必要な資金を引いた、フリーキャッシュフローから充当される。

財務改善
financial improvement
財務内容の良くない企業が抱える課題のひとつ。借入金の返済などにより、財務体質を強化することを指す。株主還元と同様、フリーキャッシュフローが充当される。

TRANSLATION

小浜教授：ところで、キャッシュフロー経営って知ってるかい？

マキ：え～、分かりません。でも、名前からしてキャッシュフローを重視した経営のことですか？

小浜：そう。キャッシュフロー経営の基本は、「稼ぐ」と「使う」なんだよ。つまり、企業は「営業キャッシュフロー」で稼いで、その額を超えないように「投資キャッシュフロー」と「財務キャッシュフロー」を制限して使えばいいってこと。それだけだよ。

マキ：論理的ですよね。稼いだお金以上に使えば、赤字になっちゃいますから。

小浜：ただ、企業が現在の事業を維持しつつ将来の発展を目指すには、金の使い方、中でも「未来投資」が大切なんだ。未来投資には、設備投資だけでなく人材育成などの人への投資も含まれる。それは会社の改善向上につながるからね。未来投資のほかにも、株価を維持する上で「株主還元」ももちろん大切だし、財務内容がよくない会社は、稼いだキャッシュフローを使って「財務改善」を優先しなくてはならない。

マキ：それで、そうしたことに使うお金は、稼いだ営業キャッシュフローの中から調達するのがベスト、ということですね。じゃあ、営業キャッシュフローをいかに多く稼げるかが経営のポイントといえますね。

● Chapter 3　21日目

Obama: Exactly. More strictly speaking, the important point is how to secure "freely usable money", which is calculated by subtracting the money required for maintaining the current business from the cash flow from operating activities. This freely usable money is called "free cash flow", and the real capacity of a company is found in the ability to earn this money.

Maki: The ability to earn is very important, isn't it? My mother always tells me to marry a man who can earn a lot of money.

Obama: Ha, ha, ha. I quite agree with her. But, as I said earlier, earning is not enough. To increase the ability to spend also increases a company's value. Even if your husband earns a lot of money, your life will be tough if he wastes it.

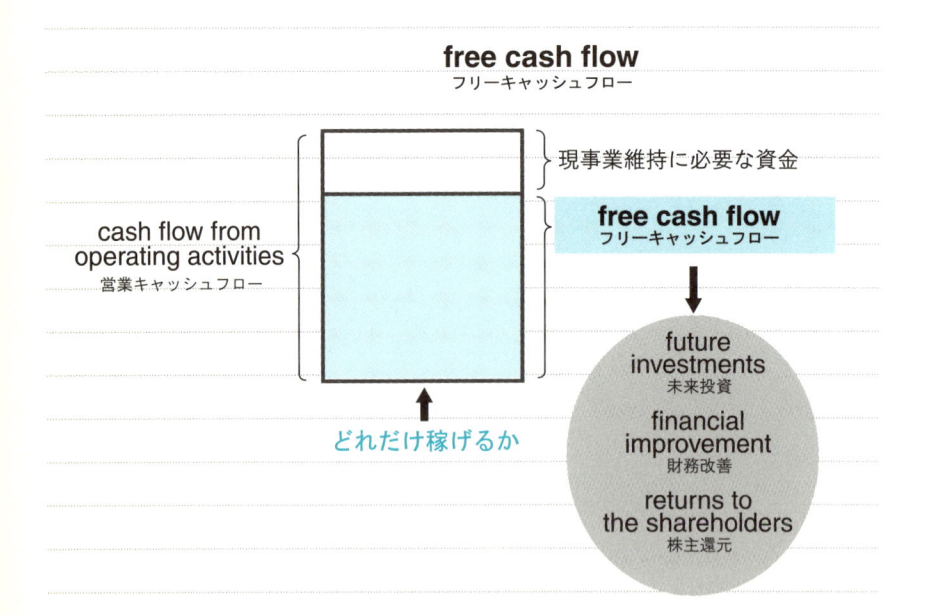

free cash flow
フリーキャッシュフロー

現事業維持に必要な資金

cash flow from operating activities
営業キャッシュフロー

free cash flow
フリーキャッシュフロー

どれだけ稼げるか

future investments
未来投資

financial improvement
財務改善

returns to the shareholders
株主還元

KEYWORDS

自由に使えるお金／フリーキャッシュフロー
freely usable money / free cash flow

営業キャッシュフローから現事業維持のために必要な資金を引いたもので、企業の真の実力を示す。本来的には、ここから未来投資・財務改善・株主還元が行われる。

小浜：その通り。もっと厳密に言えば、現事業の維持に必要な資金を営業キャッシュフローから差し引いた「自由に使えるお金」、これをどうやって確保するかが大切なんだ。この自由に使えるお金を「フリーキャッシュフロー」と言い、このお金をいかに稼げるかが、企業の真の実力と言える。

マキ：稼ぐ力って大事ですよね。母からもよく「しっかり稼ぐ人と結婚しなさい」って言われますもん。

小浜：ははは、確かに同感だね。でも、さっきも言ったように、稼ぐだけじゃ駄目。使う力を高めることも、会社の価値を高めるんだ。どんなに稼ぐ夫でも、その人に浪費癖があったら生活は結局、大変になるからね。

Words & Phrases

①②③……は、その語が登場した行数を表しています。

② emphasize　強調する
④ fundamental　基本、原則
⑫ make a loss　損失を出す
⑰ plant and equipment　生産設備
㉑ financial performance　財務実績
㉗ strictly speaking,　厳密に言えば
㉘ secure　確保する、確実に手に入れる
㊳ tough　厳しい、困難である

Chapter 3

22日目 DCFと会社の価値の上げ方

Prof. Obama: Tell me, do you know about "discounted cash flow" as a way of calculating the value of a company?

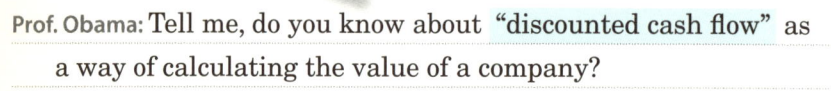

Maki: Yes, I've heard about it. But, I don't know how you calculate it.

Obama: Well, let me explain. Adjusting the future cash flows to the present value gives us what is known as "discounted cash flow", or DCF for short. And the "present value of a company" is calculated by subtracting "liabilities with interest" from DCF. Let me explain it in more detail. We forecast the future cash flow for each year and discount it by the interest. Suppose, the present cash flow is one million yen and the interest is 1%. How much will that one million yen be one year from now?

Maki: One million yen times 1.01, which is 1.01 million yen.

Obama: Right. Now, let's consider it in the opposite direction. I mean, how much will the present value of one million yen be one year from now?

Maki: One million yen divided by 1.01, means it will be about 0.99 million yen.

Obama: So, this 0.99 million yen is the "present value of one million yen one year from now".

Maki: That's the way we adjust the future value to the present value, isn't it? So, if we subtract the liabilities with interest from the present value, can we obtain the value of the company?

Obama: Well, we don't need to worry about that for the moment. But, please remember that DCF is a very important term to

KEYWORDS

ディスカウンティッド・キャッシュフロー
discounted cash flow / DCF

企業の価値（株式の価値）を計算する方法で、企業が生み出す将来のキャッシュフローを現時点の価値に直したものから、現在の有利子負債を引くことで算出される。ディスカウントキャッシュフローや、割引現在価値などとも呼ばれる。

企業価値＝「キャッシュフローの現在価値」－「有利子負債」

TRANSLATION

小浜教授：ところで、会社の価値を計算する方法として「ディスカウンティッド・キャッシュフロー」があるんだけど、知ってるかい？

マキ：ええ、聞いたことはありますが、計算方法が分からなくて。

小浜：じゃあ、簡単に説明しよう。「ディスカウンティッド・キャッシュフロー」、略してDCFは、将来のキャッシュフローを今の価値に直したもの（キャッシュフローの現在価値）だ。そして、DCFから有利子負債を引いたものが、DCFで計算する企業の価値（株式の価値）なんだ。もうちょっと詳しく説明すると将来のキャッシュフローを毎年分予測して、それを金利で割り引くってことさ。そうだな、例えば、現在100万円のキャッシュフローがあって、金利が1％だとしよう。100万円は1年後、いくらになるかな？

マキ：100 × 1.01 で101万円です。

小浜：そうだ。じゃ、これを逆に考えてみよう。つまり、1年後の100万円は、今の価値だといくらになるかな？

マキ：100 ÷ 1.01 で、約99万円です。

小浜：つまり、この約99万円が「1年後の100万円の、現在価値」というわけだ。

マキ：将来の価値を今の価値に直すって、こういうことなんですね。その現在価値から有利子負債を引くと、その会社の価値が導き出せるわけですね。

小浜：まあ、差し当たって悩まなくていいよ。でも、DCFが会社の価値を表す

show the value of a company. Now, how do you think we can increase the present value of a company?

Maki: Well, it must be a subtraction. The answer is either to increase "future cash flow" which is the amount we start with, or to decrease "liabilities with interest" which is the amount we subtract. Is that correct?

Obama: Yes, that's right. You've got it.

Maki: I see. So, if you use the money earned from cash flow from operating activities for future investments, the future cash flow will increase. On the other hand, if you use the money for loan repayments, the liabilities with interest will decrease. So, "to earn" and "to spend" will increase the value of a company. Oh, I see. I really do understand!

KEYWORDS

将来のキャッシュフロー
future cash flow
企業活動における将来の現金収入予測数値で、近年、企業価値を算出するためによく用いられるディスカウンティッド・キャッシュフロー（DCF）の元になるもの。

有利子負債
liabilities with interest
☞ 3日目、4日目、6日目

大切なものだってことは覚えておいてね。じゃあ、会社の現在の価値であるDCFを上げるには、どう計算すればいいか分かる？

マキ：え〜っと、引き算のはずだから、引かれる数の「将来のキャッシュフロー」を増やすか、引く数の「有利子負債」を減らすか、ですよね？

小浜：その通り。これで意味が分かったね。

マキ：なるほど。営業キャッシュフローで稼いだお金を未来投資に使うと、将来のキャッシュフローは増える。一方で、借入金を返済することにお金を使えば、有利子負債は減る。だから、「稼ぐ」と「使う」が、会社の価値を高める。なるほど、しっかり納得です！

Words & Phrases
①②③……は、その語が登場した行数を表しています。

⑤ adjust　調整する、適合させる
⑦ for short　略して
⑨ forecast　予測する
⑩ Suppose,　もし〜だったらどうだろう
⑬ time　（数を）〜倍する
⑭ opposite　反対の
㉓ obtain　手に入れる、獲得する
㉙ subtraction　引き算

Chapter 3

23 政府のキャッシュフロー計算書

Maki: Professor Obama, we know that a cash flow statement is regarded as quite important in the management of a company. But, how about the cash flow of the Japanese government?

Prof. Obama: The government doesn't have a cash flow statement. But, as the government budget is based on cash, it's possible to make a cash flow statement by dividing the revenues and expenditures of the general account budget into two sections: "cash flow from operating and investing activities" and "cash flow from financing activities".

　　　Let's have a look, taking the general account budget for the fiscal year 2007* as an example. Regarding "cash flow from operating and investing activities", the total amount of "tax and stamp revenues" plus "other income" in the revenue column is known as the inflow, or the income of cash flow, and that amount is 57.5 trillion yen.

　　　On the other hand, the outflow, or the expenditure, is the total of items such as "social security" and "local allocation tax grants, etc." which is about 61.9 trillion yen. Therefore, the "cash flow from operating and investing activities" is minus-4.4 trillion yen. So, the negative amount of investing activities is not covered by the cash flow from operating activities.

Maki: Wow, so the government isn't following the principle of "spending money within the cash flow generated by operating activities" which we discussed a while ago.

Obama: No, it isn't. Now, let's see the remaining cash flow from financing activities. Here, "bond issues" of 25.4 trillion yen is

KEYWORDS

一般会計予算
general account budget
国及び地方公共団体において主体となる、教育・福祉・消防など国民・住民サービスとして行われる一般事業での資金の出入り（歳入・歳出）を包括的に経理する会計。

租税及び印紙収入
tax and stamp revenues
国及び地方公共団体の歳入において最も主体となる収入。

社会保障
social security
国・社会が、疾病やけが、出産・加齢・障害・失業など生活上の問題の予防・救済・安定を目的に、所得を保障したり、医療・介護などのサービスを給付したりすること。

地方交付税交付金
local allocation tax grants
地方公共団体の税収不足の補てん、十分な行政サービスの実施、地方公共団体間の財源格差調整のために、所得税・消費税など国税五税の一部から再分配される交付金。

公債の発行（公債金収入）
bond issues
政府は、歳出に必要な資金を税収で賄うことができない場合、国債の発行を通じて資金を借り入れる。新規国債発行による資金調達は、一般会計予算における歳入の公債金収入に計上される。

TRANSLATION

マキ：小浜先生、企業経営ではキャッシュフロー計算書が重視されているわけですよね。じゃあ、日本政府のキャッシュフローはどうなってるんですか？

小浜教授：政府のキャッシュフロー計算書は作成されていないんだ。しかし政府の予算はキャッシュベースだから、一般会計予算の歳入と歳出から2つに分けて「営業＋投資キャッシュフロー」と「財務キャッシュフロー」のキャッシュフロー計算書を作ることは可能だよ。

じゃあ、平成19年度（2007年度）の一般会計予算＊を例に、実際に見てみよう。まずは「営業＋投資キャッシュフロー」だけど、歳入の中の「租税及び印紙収入」に「その他収入」を足したものが、キャッシュフローのうちのインフロー、つまり収入を表す。これが57.5兆円。

一方、アウトフロー、つまり歳出の方は、歳出の「社会保障」や「地方交付税交付金等」までを合計した約61.9兆円。従って、「営業＋投資キャッシュフロー」は、4.4兆円の赤字。だから平成19年度は、投資キャッシュフローのマイナス分を営業キャッシュフローで賄っていないのが分かるね。

マキ：うわ、さっき話した「営業キャッシュフローの範囲内で使う」っていう原則から、政府は外れているんですね。

小浜：そう、外れているんだ。じゃ、残りの財務キャッシュフローを見てよう。これは、「公債金収入」の25.4兆円がインフローで、アウトフローに相当する

＊平成19年度の一般会計予算は、68ページを参照。

the inflow, and "national debt service" is the outflow, which is 21 trillion yen. The cash flow should be negative, but it's actually positive.

Maki: Really? Could it be that the shortage of "cash flow from operating and investing activities" is covered by the cash flow from financing activities?

Obama: Exactly! As I told you earlier, "sound" cash flow management is to earn money through cash flow from operating activities and free cash flow, and to spend the money on future investments, financial improvements and returns to the shareholders. The government's fiscal condition is exactly the opposite and quite severe. They can't make any future investments or financial improvements because they don't have enough free cash flow.

Maki: Oh, I see. They can't invest, as they don't have enough cash flow. No wonder they can't proceed with the construction of the Linear Express or the Second Tomei Expressway!

Obama: Right. And, if you don't spend money on future investments, you can't expect future prosperity, as we discussed in the case of Nissan.

KEYWORDS

国債費
national debt service
満期を迎えた国債の償還金で、一般会計予算においては、歳出の国債費に示される。

のが「国債費」で21兆円。ここでも、本来マイナスであるべきところが、(4.4兆円も) プラスになっている。

マキ：あれ？　もしかして、「営業＋投資キャッシュフロー」の不足分を、財務キャッシュフローで補っちゃってるんですか？

小浜：その通り。営業キャッシュフローでお金やフリーキャッシュフローを稼いで、未来投資、財務改善、株主還元にお金を使うのが「健全な」キャッシュフロー経営だったよね。日本政府の財政は、それとは真逆を行く、相当厳しい状況だ。フリーキャッシュフローが十分でないんだから、未来投資や財務改善が進むわけがない。

マキ：そうか、キャッシュフローが十分にないから投資ができない。道理で、リニアモーターカーにしても第二東名にしても、なかなか建設が前に進んでいかないんですね！

小浜：そうそう。そして未来投資を行わなければ、日産の例で話したように、将来の繁栄は期待できないんだ。

Words & Phrases
①②③……は、その語が登場した行数を表しています。

- ① be regarded as　〜と見なされる
- ⑤ budget　予算
- ⑥ revenue　（国家の）歳入
- ⑦ expenditure　歳出
- ⑬ column　列、段、項目
- ⑯ outflow　歳出、支出
- ㉒ principle　原理、原則、正道
- ㊱ improvement　良くなること、改善
- ㊳ opposite　正反対のこと、逆のもの
- ㊳ severe　厳しい、深刻な
- ㊷ No wonder　道理で〜なわけだ
- ㊺ prosperity　繁栄、成功

Chapter 3

24日目 最優先されるべきは「人材育成」

Maki: How can the government make its fiscal condition healthier?

Prof. Obama: Well, you can take Nissan's case as an example. Mr. Ghosn hurriedly improved their financial condition first of all, to avoid bankruptcy, and then began spending money on future investments while maintaining a good balance. The government also needs to get an even primary balance first. But, on the other hand, if they don't spend enough money on future investments, it will surely have a bad effect on our future.

Maki: Well, the point is to get a good balance between the present and the future, isn't it?

Obama: Yes, the government needs to avoid useless expenditure while improving the fiscal condition, and to spend money on future investments. I think they should give top priority to the "development of human resources". "Human resources" are often called the most important resources for both companies and the Japanese government, but they are not listed as assets on the balance sheet or on the cash flow from investing activities. They are treated as "expenses".

Maki: It's true that no successful company can continue to prosper if its staff are not developed properly. Human resources are a source of future profits. I think they should be regarded as assets.

Obama: So do I. For one thing, Japan doesn't have enough resources or food, so it's not too much to say that Japan has developed to this level due to the wisdom of the people. Spending money on human resources is very important for our future development.

KEYWORDS

人材育成
development of human resources

資源・食糧に乏しい日本にとって、人材育成とそのための教育は、国家レベルでも個別企業においても最大の資源といわれる。ただし会計上、人材に関してはすべて費用として処理される。

投資キャッシュフロー
cash flow from investing activities

☞ 19日目

費用（経費）
expenses

企業が、その主たる事業活動において利益を生み出すために費やす資金。会計上は費用が正しい呼び方。

優良企業
successful company

ここでは、継続的に利益を生んでいて、財務体質もよい企業を指している。

TRANSLATION

マキ：先生、どうすれば政府は財政を健全化できるんですか？

小浜教授：そこでも日産の例を参考にすればいいんだ。ゴーンさんはまず、倒産を防ぐために財務改善を急いだ。そしてその後、バランスを取りながら未来投資をし始めたね。政府も、まずはプライマリーバランスの収支を合わせなければならない。かといって、未来投資を十分に行わないと、将来にも必ず悪影響が出てくる。

マキ：うーん。要は現在と未来のバランスをとるってことですか。

小浜：そう、政府は、ムダな支出を抑えて財政を改善しながらも、未来投資にお金を使う必要があるんだ。僕は、政府が最優先にすべきなのは「人材育成」だと思っている。「人材」というのは、企業にとっても国にとっても最大の資源と言われている。なのに、貸借対照表に資産として載ることもなければ、投資キャッシュフローにも載らず、すべて「費用」として処理されるんだ。

マキ：確かに、どんな優良企業でも、人がきちんと育っていなければ、いずれ駄目になってしまいますよね。人材は将来の収益を生む源泉なんだから、資産として見なされてもいいのに。

小浜：そうなんだ。日本は資源も食糧も乏しい。なのにここまで発展できたのは、人々の知恵のおかげといっても過

● Chapter 3　24日目

　So, from now on I'll have to be stricter when I teach you. This is a sort of human resource development.
Maki: What? That's strange logic!

■人材育成、教育こそ最大の未来投資のはずだが……
国立大学と私立大学の授業料の推移（単位：円）

年度	国立大学	私立大学
1975	36,000	182,677
1976	96,000	221,844
1979	144,000	325,198
1984	252,000	451,722
1989	339,600	570,584
1994	411,600	708,847
1999	478,800	783,298
2004	520,800	817,952

注：私立大学の額は平均値、年度は入学年度。

（出所：文部科学省）

キャッシュフロー

KEYWORDS

言ではない。だから、人材に投資することは将来の発展のために重要なことなんだ。というわけで、これからはますます厳しくマキさんを指導しないと。これも一種の人材育成だからね。

マキ：ええー？？　それは話が飛びすぎですよ！

Words & Phrases　①②③……は、その語が登場した行数を表しています。

③ hurriedly　大急ぎで
④ avoid　（好ましくないことを）回避する
⑬ give top priority to　～を最優先に扱う
⑲ prosper　繁栄する、繁盛する
⑳ staff　（企業で働く）職員集団、社員
⑳ properly　適切に、きちんと
㉕ wisdom　英知、賢明な行動

Chapter 3

REVIEW EXERCISE
Chapter 3 で学んだ内容を復習しよう

TR26 まずは、チャンツのリズムに乗せて Keywords を発音しましょう。

- **Linear Express** リニア新幹線
- **cash-in and cash-out** 現金の出入り
- **valuation loss** 評価損
- **profit on the books** 帳簿上の利益
- **accounts receivable** 売掛金
- **accounts payable** 買掛金
- **V-shaped recovery** V字回復
- **future investments** 未来投資

< pause >

- **operating activities** 営業活動
- **investing activities** 投資活動
- **financing activities** 財務活動
- **acquisition** 取得
- **tangible fixed assets** 有形固定資産
- **leased assets** リース資産
- **dividend** 配当（金）
- **capital issuance** 増資

< pause >

- **returns to the shareholders** 株主還元
- **financial improvement** 財務改善
- **free cash flow** フリーキャッシュフロー
- **discounted cash flow** ディスカウンティッド・キャッシュフロー
- **liabilities with interest** 有利子負債
- **general account budget** 一般会計予算
- **tax and stamp revenues** 租税および印紙収入
- **social security** 社会保障

< pause >

- **human resources** 人材
- **expenses** 費用（経費）
- **subtract** 差し引く
- **exceed** 上回る、超える
- **equipment** 設備、装置
- **machinery** 機械（類）
- **expenditure** 支払額、費用
- **prosperity** 繁栄

キャッシュフロー

会社の実力を英語で診断！

キャッシュフロー計算書を見て、以下の問いに答えましょう。

A社　Statement of Cash Flows

Cash flows from (①) activities	
Net profit before income taxes	2,600
Depreciation	800
Unrealized losses on marketable securities	10
・・・・・・・・・・・・・	△ 410
Net cash provided by (①) activities	3,000
Cash flows from (②) activities	
Purchase of tangible fixed assets	△ 1,000
Purchase of other investments	△ 2,000
Net cash provided by (②) activities	△ 3,000
Cash flows from (③) activities	
Increase in long-term debt	3,000
Payments of long-term debt	△ 2,000
Dividends paid	△ 500
・・・・・・・・・・・・・	
Net cash provided by (③) activities	500
Net increase (decrease) in cash and cash equivalents	500

B社　Statement of Cash Flows

Cash flows from (①) activities	
Net profit before income taxes	180
Depreciation	600
Unrealized losses on marketable securities	10
・・・・・・・・・・・・・	△ 90
Net cash provided by (①) activities	700
Cash flows from (②) activities	
Purchase of tangible fixed assets	△ 400
Purchase of other investments	500
Net cash provided by (②) activities	100
Cash flows from (③) activities	
Increase in short-term borrowings	△ 800
Increase in long-term debt	1,000
Payments of long-term debt	△ 1,000
Dividends paid	△ 100
・・・・・・・・・・・・・	
Net cash provided by (③) activities	△ 900
Net increase (decrease) in cash and cash equivalents	△ 100

問1 例題のキャッシュフロー計算書の各空欄に、区分名を入れてから訳してください。
＊A社、B社の損益計算書は、Chapter 2 の Review Exercise（p.79）にあります。

問2 会社が中長期的に成長していくために必要な投資を行っているかを判断するのに、キャッシュフロー計算書上のどの数値を見ることが有用ですか。例題の数値に基づき、両社の比較をしてください。
比較すべき数値項目：（　　　　　）≧≦（　　　　　　　）
A社：（　　　　）≧≦（　　　　　）
B社：（　　　　）≧≦（　　　　　）

問3 キャッシュフロー計算書は、3つのセクションに分かれていますが、一般的に、各セクションはどのような状態であることが望ましいでしょうか。両社について計算をして比較してください。
望ましい状態：（　　　）－{（　　　）＋（　　　）}＞0
A社：（　　　）－{（　　　）＋（　　　）}＝（　　　）
B社：（　　　）－{（　　　）＋（　　　）}＝（　　　）

解答と解説

A社　キャッシュフロー計算書	
（営業）活動からのキャッシュフロー	
税金等調整前当期純利益	2,600
減価償却費	800
有価証券評価損	10
・・・・・・・・・・・・・	△ 410
（営業）活動キャッシュフロー　小計	3,000
（投資）活動からのキャッシュフロー	
有形固定資産の購入支出	△ 1,000
その他投資資産の購入支出	△ 2,000
（投資）活動キャッシュフロー　小計	△ 3,000
（財務）活動からのキャッシュフロー	
長期借入金の増加	3,000
長期借入金の返済	△ 2,000
配当金の支払	△ 500
・・・・・・・・・・・・・	
（財務）活動キャッシュフロー　小計	500
キャッシュフロー　合計	500

B社　キャッシュフロー計算書	
（営業）活動からのキャッシュフロー	
税金等調整前当期純利益	180
減価償却費	600
有価証券評価損	10
・・・・・・・・・・・・・	△ 90
（営業）活動キャッシュフロー　小計	700
（投資）活動からのキャッシュフロー	
有形固定資産の購入支出	△ 400
有形固定資産の売却収入	500
（投資）活動キャッシュフロー　小計	100
（財務）活動からのキャッシュフロー	
短期借入金の増加	△ 800
長期借入金の増加	1,000
長期借入金の返済	△ 1,000
配当金の支払	△ 100
・・・・・・・・・・・・・	
（財務）活動キャッシュフロー　小計	△ 900
キャッシュフロー　合計	△ 100

問1　① operating：営業（活動からのキャッシュフロー）
　　　② investing：投資（活動からのキャッシュフロー）
　　　③ financing：財務（活動からのキャッシュフロー）

問2　比較すべき数値項目：「減価償却費」≧≦「有形固定資産の取得」
　　　A社：（減価償却費　800）＜（有形固定資産の取得支出　1,000）
　　　B社：（減価償却費　600）＞（有形固定資産の取得支出　　400）

問3　（営業キャッシュフロー）のプラスで、｜（投資キャッシュフロー）＋（財務キャッシュフロー）｜を合わせたマイナスをカバーする状態。
　　　A社：（3,000）＞｜(△3,000)＋(500)｜
　　　B社：(700)＜｜(100)＋(△900)｜

Chapter 3 のまとめ

●キャッシュフロー計算書（cash flow statement）とは……
利益ではなく「現金」の動きを、3つのセクションに分けて示す

「営業キャッシュフロー」「投資キャッシュフロー」「財務キャッシュフロー」の3セクション

キャッシュフロー計算書

1、 営業キャッシュフロー cash flow from **operating** activities
通常の営業活動における現金の出入り
稼ぐこと＝「プラス」が原則

2、 投資キャッシュフロー cash flow from **investing** activities
企業が投資活動を行ったことによる現金の出入り
使うこと＝「マイナス」が原則

3、 財務キャッシュフロー cash flow from **financing** activities
資金調達や株主還元といった財務活動による現金の出入り
使うこと＝「マイナス」が原則

●下線部に対応する英語を記入しながら、学習内容を最後にまとめましょう。

キャッシュフロー（現金の支出）を伴わない費用がある。

現金の支出を伴わない費用の代表選手は「評価損」と「減価償却費」

投資キャッシュフローは、人材育成も含めて「未来投資」をしているかに注目

未来投資をしている証左は「有形固定資産の取得＞減価償却費」

企業の真の実力は「自由に使えるお金」を稼げるかで決まる。

Column 3

日本企業はなぜ、高自己資本比率と低 ROE を、放置するのか？

　断っておきますが、私はスティールパートナーズのような、強行的な敵対的買収を行うやり方は日本の経営に合わないと思っています。私自身もバイアウトファンドにかかわっていますが、敵対的な買収は一切やりません。敵対的に買収しても結果的にうまくいかないだろうと思うからです。日本には日本の経営風土に根ざした日本流のやり方があります。

　だからと言って、敵対的買収はすべて悪だとも思いません。十分な資産を持ちながら有効活用できていないような非効率な経営を行っている企業が、敵対的買収などに対して緊張感を持ち、経営改善を行う努力をするのは、良いことだと思っています。そうなれば国全体の活力も上がるでしょう。

　私は、「企業の存在意義は、良い商品やサービスをお客さまに提供し、それを通じて社会に貢献すること」だと思っています。それを怠っているのでは、企業の存在意義はありません。

　ですから、そうしたより良い商品やサービスを提供することを後押しするようなプレッシャーを与えるファンドには大賛成ですし、それを阻害し、単に資産の切売りのようなことを行わせるファンドや企業買収には反対です。

　また、経営能力の低い経営者が居座るための敵対的買収防衛策などには、当然反対です。自分たちの努力や能力不足を買収防衛策でカバーするというのなら、上場を廃止して、好き勝手な経営をすればよいのです。十分なパフォーマンスも出せないでいながら、嫌な株主は除外してそれでも上場を維持したいなどという「身勝手」な考え方は、おかしいし、日本全体のためにもならないと考えます。（こ）

Chapter 4

ブランドが大好き、IT企業

コレが本当の狙い！ ―損益分岐点―

Chapter 4

26日目 新しい収益構造を持つ企業の誕生

Maki: Professor Obama, you like baseball, don't you? Did you catch yesterday's baseball game on TV?

Prof. Obama: Yes, it was a great game. But I didn't know you liked baseball so much.

Maki: I like a lot of sports. I only watch though. You know, I've noticed that in the last few years, IT companies like Rakuten and SoftBank have been buying professional baseball teams. Livedoor was also trying to buy the Kintetsu Buffaloes. Why do IT companies want to own baseball teams? Is running a baseball team particularly profitable?

Obama: Well, if we only consider whether it's profitable or not, then, no, it isn't. At least, it's not easy to make a profit.

Maki: Then, why have they been buying baseball teams? Surely their money would be better spent investing in a related business or buying a company with a sure profit.

Obama: That would be true if they belonged to a traditional industry.

Maki: A traditional industry? Does that mean that the IT industry is different from traditional industries in some way?

Obama: Yes, the IT industry has a different profit-making mechanism than that of traditional industries. That's why IT companies want to own baseball teams.

Maki: When you say a different profit-making mechanism, you mean a different "business model", don't you? How exactly is it different from traditional models?

Obama: Well, to understand the difference, you need to know about

KEYWORDS

IT企業／IT産業
IT company / IT industry

IT企業とは、コンピューターメーカーや通信事業者、ソフトウェアメーカーなど、情報・通信技術に関連する事業を営む会社の総称。IT企業の展開する事業を総合したものがIT産業。IT産業には、コンピューターやその周辺機器の「製造」から、ソフトウェアの「開発」、ハードおよびソフトウェアの「販売」、ネットワークや通信サービス、企業の情報システムの「構築」など、非常に幅広い分野の業種が含まれる。

収益構造
profit-making mechanism

どんな事業を行い、どのように収益を上げるのかという、企業の「利益を生み出す仕組み」のこと。「ビジネスモデル」とも呼ばれる。

TRANSLATION

マキ：先生は野球がお好きですよね。昨日の試合、テレビでご覧になりました？

小浜教授：ああ、本当にいい試合だったな。それにしても、マキさんが野球好きだとは、知らなかったな。

マキ：ええ、いろいろなスポーツが好きなんです。と言っても見る方専門ですけど。そういえば先生、ここ数年、楽天やソフトバンクのような、IT企業がプロ野球チームを買っていますよね。あのライブドアも近鉄球団を狙っていたし。IT企業はどうして、プロ野球チームを持ちたがるんですか？　球団経営って、そんなに儲かるんですか？

小浜：儲かるか儲からないかだけで言えば、儲からない——いや、厳密に言うと、儲かりにくいな。

マキ：じゃあ、どうしてプロ野球チームを買っているんですか？　それだけのお金があるなら、関連事業に投資したり、確実に儲かる会社を買収したりする方が、よっぽど上手な使い方だと思うんですけど。

小浜：従来型の産業に属しているんだとしたら、確かにそうだね。

マキ：従来型の産業？　ということは、IT産業はこれまでの産業とは何か違うってことですか？

小浜：そう。IT産業は、従来型の産業とは違った収益構造を持っていて、そこに、IT企業が球団を持ちたがる理由がある。

マキ：異なる収益構造、つまり、異なる「ビジネスモデル」ってことですね！　従来のとは、具体的にどう違うんですか？

小浜：その違いを理解するためには、まず、

the profit-making mechanism of traditional industries first. Traditional industries are divided largely into two groups. One is "capital-investment-type industries", such as the steel industry and the railroad industry, that require a comparatively large amount of fixed costs, and the other type is made up of "distribution industries", such as the trading and the wholesale industries, that require a large amount of variable costs.

Keywords

設備投資型産業
capital-investment-type industry

減価償却費などの固定費が多くかかる産業。多額の初期投資を必要とするため、その巨額な設備投資が参入障壁となっている。鉄鋼業などのメーカーや電鉄、通信事業のほか、大型ショッピングセンターの運営などもこれに当たる。

固定費
fixed costs
☞ 27日目

変動費
variable costs
☞ 27日目

従来型産業の収益構造を知らなくちゃいけないね。従来型の産業は、大きく2つに分類することができる。1つは鉄鋼業や鉄道などの、固定費が比較的多くかかる「設備投資型産業」。もうひとつは、商社や卸売業などからなる流通業で、こちらは変動費が多くかかる形態だ。

Words & Phrases

①②③……は、その語が登場した行数を表しています。

① catch （番組を）見る
⑨ own 保有する、持つ
⑩ particularly 特に、格別に
⑪ consider 考慮する
⑪ profitable 利益になる、儲かる
⑮ sure profit 確かな収益
⑯ belong to ～に属する
⑯ traditional 従来型の、既存の
㉘ divide 分ける
㉙ capital investment 資本投資、設備投資
㉚ comparatively 比較的
㉜ distribution industries 流通業
㉜ wholesale 卸売り

Chapter 4

27日目 固定費と変動費 ——変動費率を低く抑えろ！

Maki: Just a moment, professor. What do you mean by "fixed costs" and "variable costs"?

Prof. Obama: Oh, yes, sorry, let me explain. "Fixed costs" are the expenses generated regardless of any increase or decrease in sales. On the other hand, "variable costs" are the expenses that do increase or decrease depending on sales. In more concrete terms, capital investments in factories and machinery, and depreciation are the fixed costs. While variable costs are the expenses for purchased materials and the power, such as electricity and gas, used.

Maki: So, to summarize your explanation, capital-investment-type industries have high fixed costs, but relatively low variable costs. While, distribution industries have high variable costs, but lower fixed costs. So, steel manufacturers and railroad companies, for example, require a great amount of capital investment, but wholesale companies do not need such a vast amount of capital investment.

Obama: Good. Now, what do you think the special features of the "profit-making mechanism" of each industry are?

Maki: Hmm. Well, first, the capital-investment-type industries have a lot of fixed costs, which means that they will easily produce a profit once the sales exceed fixed costs. Is that right?

Obama: Yes, that's pretty good. Let me add a little bit. The ratio of variable costs to sales is called the "variable ratio", and in a capital-investment-type industry, where the variable ratio is low, you can make a great profit if the sales exceed a certain

KEYWORDS

固定費
fixed costs
生産したり販売したりする数量の増減に関係なく発生する、常に必要な一定の費用。製造業では、そのかなりの部分を減価償却費が占める。

変動費
variable costs
操業度の変化につれて変動する原価費用。原材料費、燃料費のほか、人件費の一部(夜勤手当など)も含まれる。結果的には売上高に応じて増減する。

減価償却(費)
depreciation
機械や工場のように、長期にわたって使用する有形固定資産の価値(の目減り分)を、耐用年数と使用期間に応じて費用化すること。
☞ 18日目

変動比率
variable ratio
売上高に占める変動費の割合のことで、売上高変動費比率とも呼ばれる。設備投資型産業では通常この数字が低い。
〔変動比率=変動費÷売上高〕

TRANSLATION

マキ:ちょっと待ってください、先生。そもそも「固定費」と「変動費」って何ですか?

小浜教授:ああ、そうか、すまん。まずそれを説明しよう。「固定費」とは、売上高の増減に関係なく発生する費用のこと。一方の「変動費」というのは、売上高に応じて増減する費用のことだ。具体的には、工場や機械の設備投資の減価償却費などが固定費で、変動費は、仕入れた原材料や、使用した電力やガスなどの費用のことだよ。

マキ:じゃあ、先生の説明を要約すると、設備投資型産業は、固定費が多くかかるけれど、変動費は比較的少なくて済む産業。反対に、流通業は、固定費がそれほどかからないけれど、変動費を多く必要とする産業、ということですね。確かに、鉄鋼メーカーや鉄道会社だったら、設備投資が膨大にかかるけど、卸売の会社は、それほど多くの設備投資が要るわけじゃないですよね。

小浜:その通り! じゃあ、それぞれの産業の「収益構造」の特徴を考えてみてごらん。

マキ:うーん。えーと、まず、設備投資型産業は固定費が多くかかる。ということは、いったんその固定費より売上高が大きくなれば、利益が出やすい。そうですか?

小浜:おっ、なかなかいい線いっているよ。少し補足すると、売上高に占める変動費の割合を「変動比率」と言うんだけど、この変動比率が低い設備投資型産業の事業は、売上高がある一定値を超える

● Chapter 4   27日目

amount.

Maki: If the sales exceed a certain amount?

Obama: Yes, to be precise, it's the sales amount which is equal to the cost. It is called the "break-even point of sales". In a capital-investment-type industry which requires a great amount of fixed costs, it is hard to reach the break-even point. But, once sales exceed that point, it will produce an enormous amount of profit because the variable costs are small.

Maki: So, in a distribution industry where the variable costs are high, it's pretty difficult to make a big profit even if the sales value goes above the break-even point because the variable costs also increase.

Obama: Yes, that's right! It's true that distribution industries don't produce big profits. But because they don't require much capital investment, entering the market is easy, and competition is hard. That is a feature of distribution industries. On the other hand, a capital-investment-type industry requires an enormous amount of money to enter the market, which becomes a barrier and limits the number of players in the market.

Maki: Oh, I see.

設備投資型産業と流通業の収益構造の違い

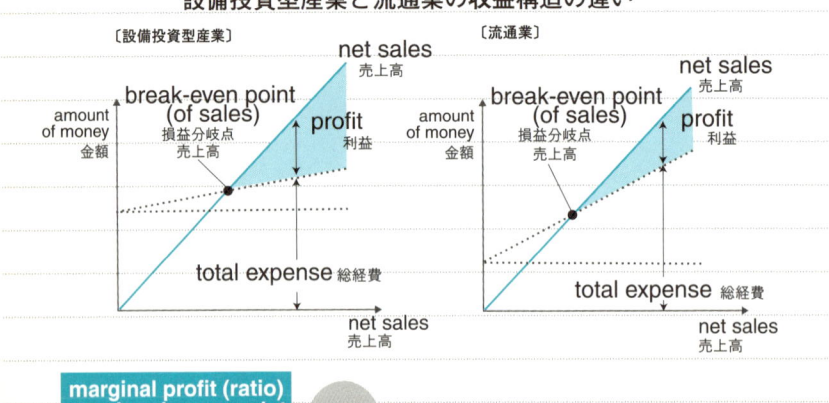

〔設備投資型産業〕

amount of money 金額 — break-even point (of sales) 損益分岐点 売上高 — net sales 売上高 — profit 利益 — total expense 総経費 — net sales 売上高

〔流通業〕

amount of money 金額 — break-even point (of sales) 損益分岐点 売上高 — net sales 売上高 — profit 利益 — total expense 総経費 — net sales 売上高

marginal profit (ratio) over break-even point 損益分岐点を超えた場合の利益率   高   低

KEYWORDS

損益分岐点（売上高）
break-even point (of sales)

売上高とそれを得るのに要した費用が一致するところ（での売上高）。変動比率の低い産業では、売上高がこの損益分岐点を超えると、利益が大幅に増えることになる。
☞ 9日目

と、すごく儲かるんだ。

マキ：売上高がある一定の値を超えると、ですか。

小浜：そう、正確に言えば、売上高と費用が一致する売上高のこと。これを「損益分岐点（売上高）」と呼ぶんだ。設備投資型産業は固定費が多くかかるから、なかなか損益分岐点に達しない。だけど、いったん売上高がこれを超えてしまえば、変動費が少ないから、後は膨大な利益が出ることになる。

マキ：なるほど。じゃあ、変動費が多くかかる流通業では、損益分岐点を超えてたくさん売れても、その分費用が増えちゃうから、大きな利益を出すのはなかなか難しいってことですか？

小浜：まさにその通り！　確かに流通業は、大きな儲けは見込めないけど、設備投資がかからない分、参入が簡単で、競争が激しい。これが流通業の特徴だ。逆に設備投資型産業は、参入するのに巨額な資金が必要だから、それが障壁となって、プレーヤーが限られる、ということだね。

マキ：なるほど。

Words & Phrases

①②③……は、その語が登場した行数を表しています。

② variable　変動する
④ generate　生み出す
④ regardless of　〜にかかわらず
⑥ concrete　具体的な、明確な
⑪ summarize　要約する
⑭ steel manufacturer　鉄鋼メーカー
㉒ exceed　超える、超過する
㉙ to be precise　正確に言うと
㉙ equal to　〜に等しい
㉝ enormous　巨大な、膨大な
㊱ sales value　売却価格
㊴ distribution industry　流通業
㊶ competition　競争
㊷ feature　特徴、特性
㊺ barrier　障害物、障壁
㊺ limit　制限する

Chapter 4

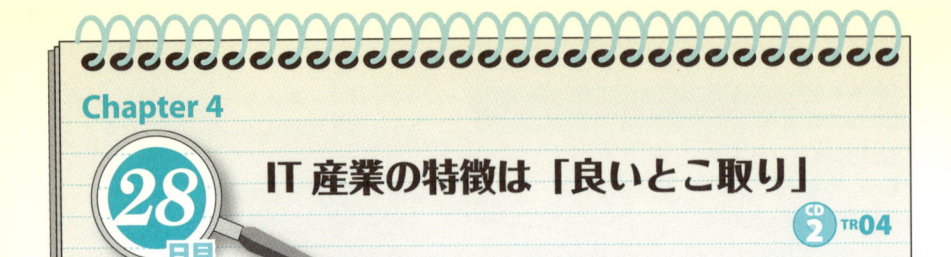

28日目 IT産業の特徴は「良いとこ取り」

Maki: Well then, professor, what's the profit-making mechanism of the IT industry? In terms of fixed costs, the main investments are mostly limited to PCs and offices, while on the other hand, the variable costs don't seem to be high.

Prof. Obama: That's right. The IT industry has very low fixed costs and very low variable costs.

Maki: Then, it's only taking the good points of traditional industries!

Obama: Yes. Regarding capital investment, virtual space is the main place of activity, so, the industry doesn't need to spend a lot on fixed costs for land and construction. In the IT industry, the barriers to entering the market are low, and it's easy to reach the break-even point. So, it's a business model that can produce big profits once it exceeds the break-even point.

Maki: When you say big profits, how much do you mean?

Obama: Well, in the case of Rakuten, their main business is operating a "virtual shopping mall" on the Internet. In this mall, there are more than 10,000 shops. If you operated an actual shopping mall, you would need an enormous amount of capital investment for land and buildings. But the virtual shopping mall on the Internet will probably need only one fiftieth or sixtieth of the capital investment needed for the traditional business. Furthermore, even if an additional shop is opened, there is no extra cost for construction, and almost no additional variable cost.

So when we look at the "virtual shopping mall" of Rakuten,

KEYWORDS

設備投資
investment
企業が建物や機械などの生産設備を新増設するために行う投資。capital investment、investment in facilities、invest in plant and machinery、equipment investment、capital expenditure など、さまざまな呼び方がある。

バーチャル空間
virtual space
実在しない概念上の空間。インターネット上で展開される商店や、ゲームの世界などを指す。仮想空間と同じ。

参入障壁
barrier to entering
新規企業が、ある産業や市場に進出しようとしたときに受ける困難（の要因）。既存産業や企業などとの相対的な関係で生じる要因を指す。entry barrier。

TRANSLATION

マキ：じゃあ先生、IT産業の収益構造ってどうなっているんですか？ 固定費のことを考えたら、主な設備投資はパソコンとオフィスだけで済んじゃうイメージだし、だからと言って変動費が多くかかるわけでもなさそうだし。

小浜教授：その通り、IT産業は固定費も変動費も非常に少なくてすむ産業ということだ。

マキ：じゃあ、従来型産業のおいしいとこ取りじゃないですか！

小浜：そう。設備投資に関しては、バーチャル空間が活動の舞台だから、土地代や建設費などに使う固定費が少なくて済む。IT産業は、参入障壁が低く、損益分岐点（売上高）まで達しやすいと言えるんだ。だから、いったん損益分岐点を超えると、大きな利益を生み出すことができるビジネスモデルなんだよ。

マキ：でも、大きな利益って言っても、どれくらい儲かるものなんですか？

小浜：例えば楽天は、ネット上の「仮想商店街」での取引がビジネスの中心で、この商店街には一万以上の店舗が出店しているね。これを本物のショッピングモールでやるとしたら、土地や建物にそれこそ膨大な設備投資費がかかってしまう。ところがインターネット上の仮想空間でだから、設備投資費は、従来型のビジネスの数十分の一程度で済んでいるだろう。しかも、参加店舗が１つ増えるからといって建て増しする必要はないから、変動費もほとんどかからないと言っていい。

　だから楽天は、「仮想商店街」ビジネ

their operating profit ratio is as much as 25% in the nine-month period of January to September for fiscal year 2007.

Maki: That's great! I'm going to start a business in the IT industry!

Obama: Just a minute. There are already so many competitors in the IT industry. How are you going to compete with them?

Maki: Let's see. If you have a unique selling point that your competitors don't have, you can differentiate yourself from them.

Obama: Yes, it's very important to have a "distinct feature" and become known for it. Do you know how to get known?

Maki: Oh, right, so that's why Rakuten wanted to buy a professional baseball team.

Obama: Exactly! One way to differentiate yourself from your competitors is by using "publicity". In the IT industry, when your customers buy products or shares of stock on the Internet, they may feel insecure. If an IT company is somewhat famous, consumers can feel secure when they do business with them. There are many ways to increase publicity. Having a professional baseball team is one of the most effective ways in Japan.

fixed cost 固定費	小
variable cost 変動費	小
break-even point (of sales) 損益分岐点売上高	低
marginal profit (ratio) over break-even point 損益分岐点を超えた場合の利益率	高

→ **low entry barrier** 低い参入障壁
high marginal profit 高い利益

KEYWORDS

売上高営業利益率
operating profit ratio

売上高に占める営業利益の割合のこと。operating margin とも呼ばれる。
〔売上高営業利益率＝営業利益÷売上高〕

知名度
publicity

広く一般に「よいイメージ」で知られていることは、消費者の信用につながる。従って、知名度を上げることは、効率のよい広告・宣伝活動だといえる。

IT産業の損益分岐点を分析すると……

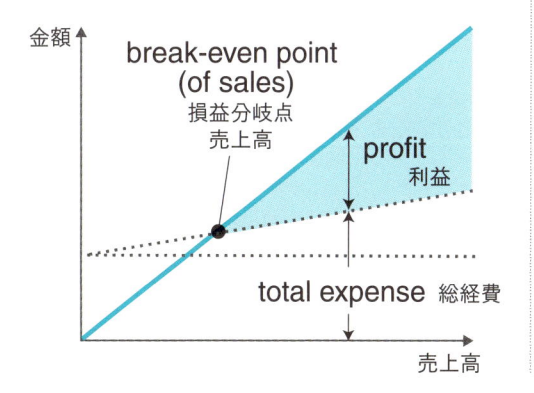

金額
break-even point (of sales)
損益分岐点売上高
profit 利益
total expense 総経費
売上高

スだけで、2007年度1-9月期決算での売上高営業利益率が、なんと、25％もあるんだ。

マキ：す、すごい！ 私、将来IT業界で起業します！

小浜：おいおい。IT業界には既にライバルがたくさんいるぞ。そのライバルにはどう対抗するつもりかい？

マキ：そうですね。何かライバルたちにはない目立った特徴があれば、他社との差別化が図れますよね。

小浜：そう、「目立った特徴」があって、人に知られるようになることが大切なんだ。人に知られるにはどんな方法があるかな？

マキ：あ、そうか、だから楽天は、プロ野球チームを持ちたがったんですね！

小浜：その通り！ 自社を競合他社と差別化する方法として「知名度」が使われるんだ。IT産業では、ネット上で商品を買ったり、株式を取引したりする場合、消費者は不安を感じることがあるだろう。そういうとき、ある程度「有名な」IT企業なら、安心感があって消費者も利用しやすい。知名度を上げる方法にはいろいろあるだろうけど、プロ野球チームを持つことは、日本では最高に効果的なもののひとつだと言えるね。

Words & Phrases
①②③……は、その語が登場した行数を表しています。

- ② in terms of 〜の観点から
- ⑨ regarding 〜に関して
- ⑪ construction （建物などの）建設
- ⑯ operate 運営する、経営する
- ⑰ virtual shopping mall 仮想商店街
- ⑱ actual 実在の、現実の
- ㉓ furthermore さらに、その上
- ㉚ competitor 競争相手、競合他社
- ㉝ differentiate 差別化する、区別する
- ㉞ distinct 際立った、目立つ
- ㉞ feature 特徴
- ㉟ get known 知られるようになる
- ㊵ customer 顧客
- ㊶ insecure 安全でない、不安な
- ㊶ somewhat いくらか、ちょっと
- ㊶ consumer 消費者

Chapter 4

29日目 固定費も変動費も少なくて済む事業を求めて

Maki: I can't think of any traditional business with low fixed costs and low variable costs.

Prof. Obama: Well, there are some. There are consultants and law offices. Pottery-making and painting are more or less the same. But, of course, these businesses have their weak points too.

Maki: So, what are their weak points?

Obama: They're businesses that you can't make too large. There's no economy of scale. Even if you want to make your business larger, it'll still require a lot of management costs or increased fixed costs.

Maki: I see. So, if you start an IT business on a small scale and expand it later, it's a dream business, isn't it?

Obama: Only if you're very successful.

Maki: I heard that trading companies have been making huge profits lately, but they're classed as a distribution industry, aren't they? I thought distribution industries didn't make a great profit because they have a lot of variable costs.

Obama: Sure, I mentioned trading companies as an example of a type of distribution industry. But, the business model of modern trading companies is different from that of traditional trading companies. Therefore, modern trading companies are exceptions among the distribution industries.

Maki: So, what is the traditional business of a trading company?

Obama: The original business of a trading company is the agent business, which is to buy the products of other manufacturers and distribute them to somebody else. But, recently, a lot of

KEYWORDS

コンサルティング会社
consultant
専門家の立場から、企業経営などについて相談に乗ったり、経営診断や助言・指導を行ったり、企画立案や問題解決を手伝ったりする会社。

規模のメリット
economy of scale
生産規模を拡大することによって製造原価が下がり、利益を増すことができること。スケールメリット。

商社
trading company
もともとは、輸出入貿易業務を中心として、商業を営む会社。国の内外に取引市場を持ち、多様な商品を取り扱う大規模な商社を総合商社と呼ぶ。商社は近年、物の流通にとどまらず、投資業務も幅広く展開している。

TRANSLATION

マキ：従来からあるビジネスで、固定費も変動費も少なくて儲かるものなんて、やっぱりないんですね。

小浜教授：いや、いくつかあるよ。例えば、コンサルティング会社や弁護士事務所。陶芸とか絵画制作もこれに近いかな。しかし、これらのビジネスにも、もちろん弱点があるんだよ。

マキ：じゃあ、それってどんな弱点なんですか？

小浜：あまり大きくできない事業だということだ。大きくしても、それほど規模のメリットが利かなかったり、事業を拡大しようとしたところで、やっぱり多くの管理コストや割増しの固定費がかかったりするからね。

マキ：うーん。そうだとするとなおさら、小規模で始めて後から大きくすることもできるIT産業は、夢のビジネスなんですね。

小浜：あくまで「当たれば」の話だよ。

マキ：最近は商社がとても儲かっているって聞いたんですけど。でも、商社って流通業に入りますよね？ 流通業は変動費が多くかかるから、大きくは儲からないんじゃなかったですか？

小浜：確かに、流通業の例として前に商社の話をしたけれど、現在の商社のビジネスモデルは、伝統的な商社ビジネスとは変わってきているんだ。だから今の商社は、流通業の中でも例外だね。

マキ：じゃあ、伝統的な商社ビジネスって、どんなものなんですか？

小浜：商社のビジネスはもともと、他社メーカーの作った製品を買って他に流通させる、右から左に流す仲介業だったんだ。しかし最近は多くの総合商社

trading companies have been shifting their business from distribution to investment in other businesses and companies.

Maki: Really? So that's why a trading company makes a profit, because their profit mechanism is similar to the IT industry, isn't it?

Obama: No, not really. The reason a trading company makes a profit is that its profit-making mechanism matches the industry in which the trading company has invested.

Maki: Matches the industry? What does that mean?

Obama: If a trading company invests in a capital-investment-type industry, its profit mechanism will be similar to that of the capital investment-type industry. And, an investment in an IT industry will produce similar returns to those obtained by the profit-making mechanism of the IT industry. For example, the energy divisions of some trading companies have recently made a great profit. The energy business is rather similar to a capital-investment-type industry. With the recent energy price hikes, the energy divisions have made much greater sales, exceeding the break-even point. Therefore, it has become possible for some trading companies to make enormous profits.

Maki: I see. Depending upon the company in which they invest, their profit mechanism changes accordingly.

KEYWORDS

設備投資型産業
capital-investment-type industry
☞ 26日目

capital-investment-type industries
〔設備投資型産業〕

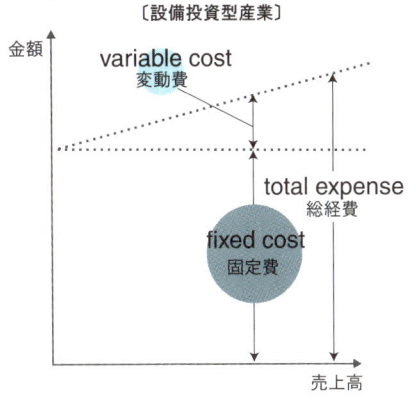

金額 / variable cost 変動費 / total expense 総経費 / fixed cost 固定費 / 売上高

distribution industries
〔流通業〕

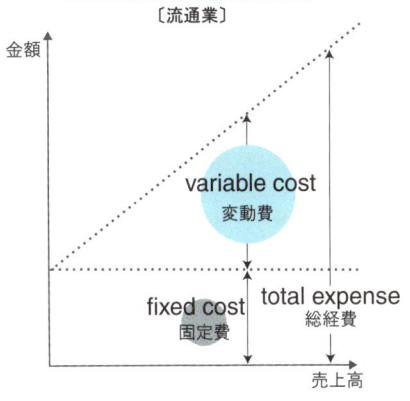

金額 / variable cost 変動費 / total expense 総経費 / fixed cost 固定費 / 売上高

が、流通から、ビジネスや企業への投資へと業務をシフトしている。

マキ：へぇー！ じゃあ商社は、IT 産業と同じような収益構造になったから儲かっている、ってわけですね！

小浜：いや、そうではない。商社が儲かっているのは、その収益構造が、投資した企業の産業形態に合致したものになるからなんだ。

マキ：産業に合致する？ どういうことですか？

小浜：設備投資型産業に投資すれば、設備投資型産業の収益構造に似てくるし、IT 型産業への投資は IT 産業の収益構造に似たリターンを生む、ということさ。例えば、いくつかの商社では最近、エネルギー部門が利益を多く上げているんだが、エネルギー事業はどちらかというと、設備投資型産業に近い。近年のエネルギー価格の上昇も相まって、エネルギー部門では損益分岐点を大きく超える売上高が生み出されて、その結果、商社が多額の利益を手にすることが可能になっているんだ。

マキ：なるほど！ 投資する企業によって、それに応じて収益構造も変化するってことなんですね。

Words & Phrases
①②③……は、その語が登場した行数を表しています。

- ③ law office　法律事務所
- ④ pottery　陶磁器、焼き物
- ④ more or less　多かれ少なかれ
- ⑬ successful　うまくやる、成功する
- ⑮ class　分類する
- ⑱ mention　述べる
- ㉒ exception　例外、特例
- ㉔ agent business　代理業務、仲介業
- ㉝ match　合致する
- ㊷ rather　かなり、相当に
- ㊹ hike　値上げ
- ㊽ accordingly　それ相応に

Chapter 4

30日目 なぜ、航空券には格安チケットがあるのか？

Prof. Obama: I believe you now have a fairly deep understanding of fixed costs and variable costs.

Maki: Yes, I think so too. By the way, Professor Obama, there's something I've been dying to know.

Obama: What's that?

Maki: The railroad, airline and hotel businesses are all capital-investment-type industries, aren't they? So, why do these businesses sell their discount tickets at different times? Airline companies sell their discount tickets from the beginning, while hotels don't give room discounts until the last minute. And *Shinkansen* give almost no discounts.

Obama: To understand the reasons, you need to know about the idea of fixed costs and variable costs for an airline company.

Maki: Is the idea of fixed costs and variable costs different for airlines?

Obama: It's not entirely different, but it is somewhat characteristic. In the case of an airline company, fuel charges and the like increase each time the airline company operates an airplane. This cost is counted as a variable cost for the company as a whole. But, when we see each airplane as a unit, the cost does not change regardless of the number of seats, therefore, it's a fixed cost.

Maki: The cost of operating an airplane can be either a fixed cost or a variable cost depending upon your viewpoint. So, how do you calculate the break-even point?

Obama: Even if an airplane is regarded as a variable cost when

KEYWORDS

損益分岐点
break-even point

break-even だけで break-even point（損益分岐点）を指すこともある。

☞ 27 日目

航空会社全体だと変動費だが、一機ごとでは固定費

for each airline
〔航空会社全体だと〕

費用

the cost increases as the number of flights increases

フライト数が増えると費用は増える

variable cost 変動費

フライト数

for each flight
〔一機ごとだと〕

費用

the cost does not change as the number of passengers increases

乗客数が増えても費用は変わらない

fixed cost 固定費

乗客数

TRANSLATION

小浜教授：固定費と変動費に関しては随分、理解が深まったと思うけど、どうだい？

マキ：はい、そう思います。ところで先生、どうしても知りたいと思っていたことがあるんですけど。

小浜：なんだい？

マキ：鉄道も航空もホテルも、みんな設備投資型産業ですよね？ じゃあ、同じ設備投資型産業なのに、どうしてばらばらのタイミングで格安チケットを売っているんですか？ 航空会社は初めから格安航空券を売っている。でも、ホテル業界はギリギリにならないと宿泊費を下げない。新幹線にいたっては、ほとんど割引はしないですよね。

小浜：その理由を理解するにはまず、航空会社の固定費と変動費の考え方を知らなくちゃ。

マキ：航空会社って、固定費と変動費の考え方が、ほかと違うんですか？

小浜：まったく違うわけじゃないんだけど、ちょっと特徴的なんだ。というのも、航空会社の場合、燃料費などは飛行機を1機飛ばすごとに増えるから、会社全体で見たときは、その費用は変動費として計算される。でも、飛行機1機単位で見たときは、座席数がいくつであっても費用は変わらないから、その費用はつまり、固定費になる。

マキ：同じ飛行機を飛ばすのに、見方によってその費用が、固定費にも変動費にもなっちゃうんですね。じゃあ、損益分岐点はどうやって出すんですか？

小浜：会社全体で見た場合には変動費であったとしても、いったん飛ばすと決

looking at the company as a whole, once they decide to operate it, the fuel charge, the crew's salary and the like will be fixed costs; because the fuel charge and the number of crew members do not change for each airplane. So, the important thing is to secure the number of passengers required to reach the break-even point for each airplane.

Maki: Oh, I see. Their aim is to secure the right number of passengers even if it means giving discounts from the beginning. But, in that case, why don't they sell tickets at the regular price first, and then sell the remaining tickets at a discount at the last minute or on the departure date?

Obama: Because you can't cancel or change your flight with a discount ticket, unlike regular tickets that do allow you to. So, by making the ticket non-exchangeable, you can secure passengers who won't change to other airlines or other flights. Thus, they secure a certain number of passengers by early purchase or by group bookings. Then, as the departure date approaches, they sell the tickets at a smaller discount or at the regular price. That's the discount system that airlines use.

Maki: It's true that a person who has to fly on a particular flight will buy the ticket even if the price is high. So, the system makes sense.

Obama: That's right. Using this system, the fixed costs and the variable costs don't change, and a "pure" profit is made with the increase of sales. This pure profit is called "marginal profit".

KEYWORDS

増し分
marginal profit

固定費が変わらず、変動費もほとんど変わらないところで上がる売上げ。詳しくは、32日目の小浜教授の説明参照。

めたら、燃料代や乗務員の給与などの費用は固定費になる。1機ごとにかかる燃料費や必要な乗員数が変わるわけではないからね。だから、とにかく大事なのは、1機ごとに損益分岐点に達するまでの乗客数を確保することだ。

マキ：なるほど。初めから安くしてでも、それだけの数を確保しようという狙いですね！ でもそれなら、初めは正規運賃で販売して、直前や出発当日になったら余りを割引いて売り出すっていう方法でもいいと思うんですけど。

小浜：しかし、飛行機の格安チケットは、正規運賃のチケットとは違って、キャンセルや便の変更ができない。つまりチケットを変更不可能にすることで、他社や他の便に変更できない乗客が確保できるんだ。そうやって一定数の乗客を早期購入や団体客でまず確保する。そして、出発日が近づくにつれて割引率の小さいチケットを売ったり、正規料金のチケットを販売したりする。これが航空会社の割引システムさ。

マキ：確かに、どうしてもその便に乗らなくちゃいけない人は、値段が高くてもそのチケットを買いますもんね。理にかなってますね。

小浜：そうなんだ。こういう仕組みで、固定費と変動費が変わらない状態で、売上だけが増えて、"おいしい"利益が得られるんだ。この"おいしい"利益を「増し分」というんだ。

Words & Phrases   ①②③……は、その語が登場した行数を表しています。

① fairly　かなり、相当に
④ be dying to　どうしても〜したい
⑯ characteristic　特徴のある、独特の
⑰ fuel charge　燃料費
⑱ operate　（飛行機を）運航する
㉔ viewpoint　見方、観点
㉘ crew　乗組員、乗務員
㉛ passenger　乗客、旅客
㉜ break-even　収支とんとんの、損益なしの
㉝ aim　狙い、目的
㉟ regular price　定価、正規の値段
㊲ departure　出発⇔arrival
㊵ exchangeable　交換可能な
㊷ purchase　購入
㊸ booking　予約

Chapter 4

31日目　割引販売のない新幹線

Maki: So, can you tell me why there is almost never a discount on *shinkansen* tickets? JR belongs to the same capital-investment-type industry as the airlines, and it's the same in that there are almost no variable costs regardless of the number of passengers. So, wouldn't it be better for JR to sell the tickets at a discount and secure the passengers as soon as possible, so that it reaches the break-even point and covers the fixed cost?

Prof. Obama: You're right. But, there is one point where JR is different. The hint is "competition". What do you think?

Maki: "Competition"? Well, there are two major airlines: JAL and ANA in the airline industry, but the *shinkansen* are only operated by JR … Ah, the airline industry gives the discount because there is competition, but there is no need for the *shinkansen* to do so because JR has a monopoly. That's why JR gives almost no discount.

Obama: Right. There is one more thing regarding discounts. "Competition" in the same traditional industry can be different. Depending on the competitive environment, the airline ticket is cheaper when it's bought early, while the hotel room tends to be cheaper with a last-minute reservation.

Maki: In other words, there are only two choices in the airline industry, but there are quite a few competitors in the hotel industry.

Obama: Yes, that's the important point. In the case of an airplane, the passenger who has to use it has to buy the ticket even if the airfare is expensive. But, there are many competitors in

KEYWORDS

競争
competition
産業も企業も、自由で公正な「競争」で育つ。そのため、寡占や談合、カルテルといった自由な競争を妨げる行為は、厳しく取り締まられる。

独占状態
monopoly
特定の資本や企業が、競争相手が不在である（あるいは排除された）ために、市場や生産を独占している状態のこと。ちなみに、独占禁止法（の総称）は antimonopoly law。

TRANSLATION

マキ：じゃあ先生、新幹線に割引がほとんどないのはどうしてなんですか？ JRも、航空会社と同じ設備投資型産業に属していて、乗客数が増えても変動費がほとんどかからない点も同じですよね。だったらJRだって、損益分岐点に到達して固定費をカバーするために、割引販売をしてお客さんを早く確保した方がいいんじゃないですか？

小浜教授：その通りさ。でも、JRには1つ違うところがあるんだ。ヒントは「競争」なんだけど、どうかな？

マキ：「競争」？ うーん、航空業界にはJALとANAという大手の2社があるけど、新幹線を運行しているのはJRだけだから……あっ、航空業界は競争があるから割引をするけど、新幹線はJRの独占状態だからその必要がない。だからJRは割引をほとんどしないんだ。

小浜：そういうこと。割引に関してはもうひとつ。同じ従来型産業での「競争」でも違うことがある。競争の環境によって、航空券は早く買う方が安いのに、ホテルの部屋は、ギリギリで予約した方が安くなりがちなんだ。

マキ：つまり、航空業界は実際のところ2社しか選択の余地がない。だけど、ホテル業界には競争相手がかなりたくさんいますよね。

小浜：そう、そこが大事。飛行機の場合、その便を使うしかない乗客は、運賃が高かろうと、そのチケットを買わざるを得ない。ところが、ホテル業界は競合相手も多く、競争がとても激しい。

the hotel industry, and the competition is very severe. When a hotel has vacancies, it's quite likely that other hotels have vacancies too. The severe competition remains the same until the last minute. Therefore, some hotels try to get hotel guests at a greatly discounted price on the very last day.

Maki: In any industry, the price is set according to the "competitive environment". Hmm, it's well arranged after all.

Obama: Just for your information, some hotels have recently started offering a "day use" service. Have you heard about it?

Maki: No, but I guess it means that customers only use it during the daytime.

Obama: Yes, that's right. Hotel rooms are mainly for accommodation, and so quite often they're not used in the daytime. That's why the "day use" method was invented. A hotel's `variable costs` are mostly bed-making expense, cleaning `personnel expenses` and amenity expenses. Therefore, if they offer the rooms for "day use", the sales will be almost all profit.

KEYWORDS

変動費
variable costs
☞ 26日目

人件費
personnel expenses
人の労働に対して支払われる費用（給料や手当）。製造に直接携わらない人の人件費は、販売費及び一般管理費として扱われる。

あるホテルに空き部屋があるときは、ほかのホテルにも空きがあることが多いから、ギリギリになっても競争は激しいままで続く。だからいよいよ当日になると、宿泊料金を大幅に下げてでもお客さんを集めようとする。

マキ：どの業界も、それぞれの「競争事情」に合わせて価格が設定されてるわけですね！　うーん、よくできてるなあ。

小浜：ちなみに、最近ホテルは「デイユース」というサービスを始めているんだけど、聞いたことある？

マキ：いいえ。でも、日中だけ使うってことですか？

小浜：そうなんだ。ホテルは宿泊がメインだから、昼間は使われていないことが多い。そこに目を付けたのがデイユースという方法なんだ。ホテルの**変動費**は、ベッドメイクの費用や清掃の**人件費**にアメニティのコストくらいだから、昼間の空いている時間にデイユースとして部屋を提供すれば、売上はそのまま儲けになるからね。

Words & Phrases
①②③……は、その語が登場した行数を表しています。

- ⑱ environment　状況、環境
- ⑳ reservation　（乗り物などの）予約
- ㉒ quite a few　かなり多くの
- ㉘ vacancies　（座席や客室などの）空き
- ㉙ severe　厳しい、激しい
- ㉛ very last　まさに最後の
- ㊳ accommodation　宿泊施設、宿泊設備
- ㊵ method　手法、方式
- ㊶ invent　考案する、創作する
- ㊷ amenity　アメニティ、生活を楽しく快適にする設備（や施設）

Chapter 4

32 「増し分」利益を得ている業界は？

Prof. Obama: As I told you earlier, the profit that is gained where the fixed costs are the same and the variable costs are almost the same is called "marginal profit".

Maki: Is "marginal profit" limited to the hotel industry? Or, does it exist in other industries?

Obama: Oh, no, it exists in other industries too. For instance, SoftBank's White Plan is another example of marginal profit.

Maki: Really? White Plan is the service that makes inter-family calls free of charge once you've paid the basic fee, isn't it?

Obama: Yes, the telecommunications industry is an equipment industry that requires an enormous amount of capital investment, which is synonymous with a fixed-cost-type industry. Even if the number of contracted phones increases, there are almost no extra variable costs. One additional contract for a mobile phone will take only the clerical work of registration, and there is no need to increase lines. As long as the line is secured, there is almost no extra variable cost, even if you send mails or make phone calls.

Maki: True, but then, why is it that telecommunication fees were so expensive until recently?

Obama: That's because they had been charging per mail and per call so that they could recover the fixed cost of the capital investment. But, using this method, actual usage varies from month to month, and so the profit varies substantially. And that's why the telecommunications companies opted for a basic fee.

KEYWORDS

増し分
marginal profit
☞ 30日目

（定額の）基本料金
basic fee
使用の頻度にかかわらず、契約関係を維持するために支払う定額の手数料料金。basic charge や basic rate とも呼ばれる。

通話料
telecommunication fees
通話サービスを利用した「量」に基づいて請求され、支払われる金額。call charges などとも呼ばれる。

TRANSLATION

小浜教授：前にも言ったけど、こうやって、固定費は変わらず、変動費もほとんど変わらないところで得られる利益のことを「増し分」と呼ぶんだよ。

マキ：「増し分」っていうのはホテル業界に限られたものですか？ それとも、ほかの業界にもあるんですか？

小浜：いや、ほかの業界にも存在しているさ。例えば、ソフトバンクのホワイトプランも増し分なんだよ。

マキ：えっ、そうなんですか？ ホワイトプランって、定額の基本料金を払ったら、家族間の通話が無料になるっていうサービスですよね？

小浜：そう。通信産業は、多額の設備投資を必要とする装置産業、つまり固定費型産業の代名詞だ。契約台数が増えても変動費はほとんどかからない。携帯電話の契約が１台増えたところで、登録の事務処理が行われるくらいで、回線を増やす必要もない。回線さえ確保してあれば、メールだって電話だって、追加の変動費はほとんどかからないんだよ。

マキ：確かに。じゃあ、最近まで通話料があんなに高かったのはどうしてなんですか？

小浜：今までは、通話やメールの使用分に応じて使った分だけ料金を取り、それで設備投資でかかった固定費分を回収しようとしていたんだ。でもこの方式だと、月によって使用料が変わり、収益が大幅に変動することになってしまう。そこで通信事業各社が目を付けたのが基本料金なんだ。

● Chapter 4　32日目

Maki: But basic fees have been lowered quite a bit.

Obama: Yes, they have, due to the severe competition in the telecommunications industry. But, the basic fee can also be a stable source of income. It accounts for substantial sales as long as membership increases. So, they're trying hard to increase membership by lowering both the basic fee and the telecommunications fees.

Maki: I see. So, in that way, they are increasing the profit by offering attractive plans to consumers without increasing the fixed cost and the variable cost even a little. It's certainly "marginal profit".

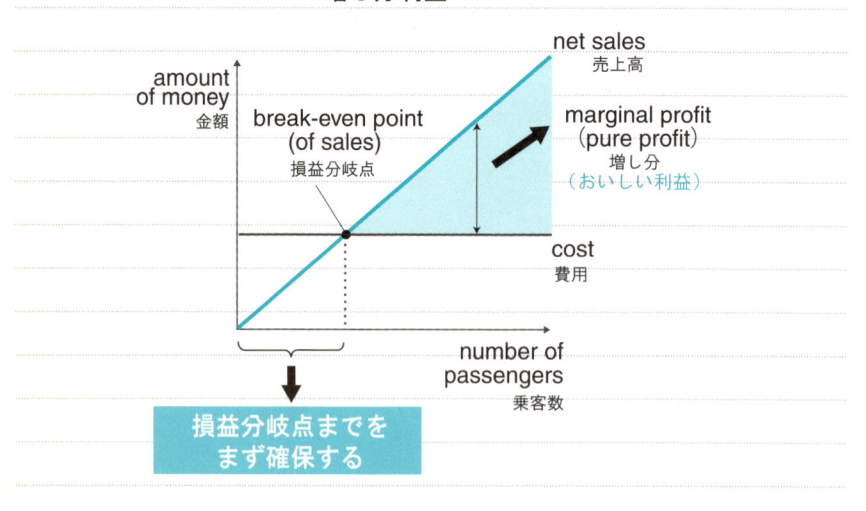

増し分利益

- amount of money 金額
- break-even point (of sales) 損益分岐点
- net sales 売上高
- marginal profit (pure profit) 増し分（おいしい利益）
- cost 費用
- number of passengers 乗客数

損益分岐点までを まず確保する

KEYWORDS

マキ：でも基本使用料も、随分安くなってきてますよ。

小浜：そう、最近は通信事業も競争が激しいからね。でも基本使用料は安定した収入になるし、加入者数が増えさえすれば、まとまった売り上げになる。だから、通信各社は、基本料金と通信料の両方を下げることで加入者数を増やそうとしているんだ。

マキ：なるほど。確かに、固定費も変動費もほとんど増やさず、消費者にとって魅力的なプランを出すだけで企業は利益を増やしている。まさに「増し分利益」ですね！

Words & Phrases
①②③……は、その語が登場した行数を表しています。

⑥ exist　存在する
⑨ free of charge　無料で
⑫ synonymous with　～と同義の
⑮ clerical　事務の、書記の
⑮ registration　登録

㉔ vary　異なる
㉔ substantially　大いに、大幅に
㉕ opt for　～を選ぶ
㉚ account for ～　～の説明となる、～を計上する

Chapter 4

33日目

REVIEW EXERCISE

Chapter 4 で学んだ内容を復習しよう

TR09 まずは、チャンツのリズムに乗せて Keywords を発音しましょう。

- profit-making mechanism
  収益構造
- fixed costs
  固定費
- variable costs
  変動費
- variable ratio
  変動比率

- break-even point
  損益分岐点
- investment
  設備投資
- virtual space
  バーチャル空間
- barrier
  障壁

< pause >

- operating profit ratio
  売上高営業利益率
- publicity
  知名度
- economy of scale
  規模のメリット
- management costs
  管理コスト

- trading company
  商社
- marginal profit
  増し分、限界利益
- competition
  競争
- monopoly
  独占状態

< pause >

- basic fee
  （定額の）基本料金
- telecommunication fees
  通話料
- distribution
  流通
- wholesale
  卸売り

- generate
  生み出す
- summarize
  要約する
- competitor
  競争相手、競合他社
- customer
  顧客

< pause >

- consumer
  消費者
- exception
  例外、特例
- agent business
  代理業務、仲介業
- hike
  値上げ

- fuel charge
  燃料費
- exchangeable
  交換可能な
- method
  手法、方式
- registration
  登録

損益分岐点

会社の実力を英語で診断！

次の損益計算書（英語版）を見ながら、以下の問いに答えましょう。

A社　Statement of Income

Net sales		26,000
Cost of sales *1		21,000
（Gross profit）		5,000
Selling and general administrative expenses *2		2,500
（Operating profit）		2,500
Non-operating income		
Interest and dividend income	100	
Other non-operating income	100	200
Non-operating expenses		
Interest expense	150	150
（Ordinary profit）		2,550
Extraordinary gains		60
Extraordinary losses		10	50
（Net profit before income taxes）		2,600
Income taxes - current		900
Income taxes - deferred	100	1,000
（Net profit）		1,600

B社　Statement of Income

Net sales		24,000
Cost of sales *1		19,500
（Gross profit）		4,500
Selling and general administrative expenses *2		4,000
（Operating profit）		500
Non-operating income		
Interest and dividend income	50	
Other non-operating income	30	80
Non-operating expenses		
Interest expense	240	240
（Ordinary profit）		340
Extraordinary gains		360
Extraordinary losses		200	160
（Net profit before income taxes）		180
Income taxes - current		70
Income taxes - deferred	0	70
（Net profit）		110

＊1　Schedule of Cost of sales（A社）

Purchase of raw material	7,000
Labor cost	9,000
Outsoucing cost	3,000
Depreciation	700
Utilities	1,300

＊2　Schedule of Selling and general administrative expenses（A社）

Personnel expenses	1,300
Utilities	100
Rent	500
Advertising	300
Depreciation	100
Telephone and postage	200

＊1　Schedule of Cost of sales（B社）

Purchase of raw material	6,700
Labor cost	9,000
Outsoucing cost	2,000
Depreciation	500
Utilities	1,300

＊2　Schedule of Selling and general administrative expenses（B社）

Personnel expenses	2,700
Utilities	100
Rent	500
Advertising	400
Depreciation	100
Telephone and postage	200

問1　例題にある損益計算書の費用を、「固定費」と「変動費」に区分してください。
　　　固定費に含まれる費用：売上原価（　　　　　　　　　　　　　　　　　）
　　　　　　　　　　　　　：販管費　（　　　　　　　　　　　　　　　　　）
　　　変動費に含まれる費用：売上原価（　　　　　　　　　　　　　　　　　）
　　　　　　　　　　　　　：販管費　（　　　　　　　　　　　　　　　　　）

問2　変動比率の計算式を英語と日本語で示し、A、B両社について計算をしてください。
　　　英（　　　　　　　　　）＝（　　　　　　　）／（　　　　　　　）
　　　日（　　　　　　　　　）＝（　　　　　　　）／（　　　　　　　）
　　　A社：（　　　　　　　）／（　　　　　　　）＝（　　　　　）
　　　B社：（　　　　　　　）／（　　　　　　　）＝（　　　　　）

問3　会社の本業の収益力を損益計算書から判断する場合、どの数値を見ればよいでしょうか。
　　　数値を使用した計算式を英語と日本語で示し、A、B両社について計算をしてください。
　　　英（　　　　　　　　　）＝（　　　　　　　）／（　　　　　　　）
　　　日（　　　　　　　　　）＝（　　　　　　　）／（　　　　　　　）
　　　A社：（　　　　　　　）／（　　　　　　　）＝（　　　　　）
　　　B社：（　　　　　　　）／（　　　　　　　）＝（　　　　　）

解答と解説

A社　損益計算書

売上高		26,000
売上原価（注1）		21,000
（売上総利益）		5,000
販売費及び一般管理費（注2）		2,500
（営業利益）		2,500
営業外収益		
受取利息及び配当金	100	
その他	100	200
営業外費用		
支払利息	150	150
（経常利益）		2,550
特別利益		60
特別損失		10	50
（税金等調整前当期純利益）		2,600
法人税、住民税及び事業税	900	
法人税等調整額	100	1,000
（当期純利益）		1,600

（注1）売上原価の内訳
- 材料仕入　　7,000
- 人件費　　　9,000
- 外注費　　　3,000
- 減価償却費　　700
- 光熱費　　　1,300

（注2）販売費及び一般管理費の内訳
- 人件費　　　1,300
- 光熱費　　　　100
- 賃借料　　　　500
- 広告宣伝費　　300
- 減価償却費　　100
- 通信運搬費　　200

B社　損益計算書

売上高		24,000
売上原価（注1）		19,500
（売上総利益）		4,500
販売費及び一般管理費（注2）		4,000
（営業利益）		500
営業外収益		
受取利息及び配当金	50	
その他	30	80
営業外費用		
支払利息	240	240
（経常利益）		340
特別利益		360
特別損失		200	160
（税金等調整前当期純利益）		180
法人税、住民税及び事業税	70	
法人税等調整額	0	70
（当期純利益）		110

（注1）売上原価の内訳
- 材料仕入　　6,700
- 人件費　　　9,000
- 外注費　　　2,000
- 減価償却費　　500
- 光熱費　　　1,300

（注2）販売費及び一般管理費の内訳
- 人件費　　　2,700
- 光熱費　　　　100
- 賃借料　　　　500
- 広告宣伝費　　400
- 減価償却費　　100
- 通信運搬費　　200

問1 固定費に含まれる費用：売上原価（Labor cost 人件費、Depreciation 減価償却費）
固定費に含まれる費用：販管費（Personnel expenses 人件費、Rent 賃借料、Depreciation 減価償却費）
変動費に含まれる費用：売上原価（Purchase of raw material 材料仕入、Outsoucing cost 外注費、Utilities 光熱費）
変動費に含まれる費用：販管費（Utilities 光熱費、Advertising 広告宣伝費、Telephone and postage 通信運搬費）

問2 英 variable ratio = variable cost ／ net sales
日（変動比率）＝（変動費）／（売上高）
A社：11,900 ÷ 26,000 ＝ 45.8%
B社：10,700 ÷ 24,000 ＝ 44.6%

問3 英 operating profit ratio = operating profit ／ net sales
日（売上高営業利益率）＝（営業利益）／（売上高）
A社：2,500 ÷ 26,000 ＝ 9.6%
B社：500 ÷ 24,000 ＝ 2.1%

Chapter 4 のまとめ

●**損益分岐点（break-even point）とは……**
売上高とそれを得るのに要した費用が一致するところ（での売上高）

設備投資型産業では
　→固定費 fixed costs が多くかかる
　　変動比率 variable ratio（変動費÷売上高）が比較的低い

　　　→ひとたび減価償却 depreciation が終われば大きな利益に！

流通業では
　→変動費 variable cost が多くかかる

増し分（利益）：固定費が変わらず、変動費もほとんど変わらないのに得られる利益

Column 4

航空機のシートピッチが新幹線より狭いのも、競争のせい？

　飛行機（特にエコノミー席）のシートピッチが狭いのに不満を持たれている方も多いと思います。それに比べて、新幹線の前席とのシートピッチは、もう少しゆったりとしています。この差は、競争の激しさの差だと考えられます。

　競争が無く許認可の状況では、「コスト＋α」で料金が決まります。もちろんJRにも競争はありますが、航空業界がさらされている競争とは比べ物になりません。

　一方、競争の激しい業界では価格競争も熾烈です。そうしたときに、効率を高くするためには、1機当たりに乗せる乗客数をできるだけ多くすることになります。それが、シートピッチに現れているのです。

　一般的には、顧客は「Q、P、S」すなわち「Quality（品質）、Price（価格）、Service（サービス）」の3つを比較して、どの会社のどの商品を選ぶかを決めると言われています。競争の激しい業界では、どうしても、QやSはより高く、Pはより低くなりがちで、そこではコスト競争力が重要となります。コストを下げなければ、同じPのまま、Q、Sをより高くしたり、従来と同じQとSをそれまでよりさらに安いPで提供したりしないといけないからです。

　そうした状況下、まだまだ高コスト体質から抜けられない日本の航空会社にとっては、今後さらなる試練の時が来るかもしれません。一方JRについては、安全性を確保した上で、JR各社の横並び意識の表れのような利益競争をやめ、「適正な」利益と「価格」「コスト構造」を作り出すような何らかのコントロールが必要でしょう。（こ）

Chapter 5

液晶テレビ、みるみる値下がり

コレがその理由だ！ —直接原価計算—

Chapter 5

34 設備投資と製品価格

Maki: Professor Obama, I've finally got an LCD television set! We bought it to get ready for terrestrial digital television broadcasting. It was much cheaper than I had expected.

Prof. Obama: Yes, prices have come down a lot. I believe you can buy a set now for less than half of what they used to be.

Maki: I know! How can manufacturers cope with lowering the price that much?

Obama: There are reasons for the low price. What do you think the reasons are?

Maki: Is it because of cutthroat competition? There were dozens of LCD TVs made by different manufacturers at the discount store.

Obama: That's one of the reasons. But, perhaps surprisingly, the "fixed costs" that we talked about before is connected with the low price; in particular, the cost needed to build factories to manufacture LCD televisions. In other words, capital investment is connected with the reason for the low price.

Maki: Oh, I'd never considered the relationship between capital investment and the product price before.

Obama: Then, first, let's think about how a company recovers the cost of capital investment.

Maki: Well, they just need to increase the product price a little bit to cover capital investment.

Obama: Exactly! But, when they add the capital investment costs to the product price, they want the added cost to be as low as possible. How can they do that?

KEYWORDS

設備投資
capital investment
☞ 28日目

TRANSLATION

マキ：先生、わが家にもとうとう液晶テレビがやってきました！　地上デジタル放送に備えて買ったんですけど、案外安いんですね。

小浜教授：ああ、大幅に値下がりして、以前の半値以下で買えるようになったんじゃないかな。

マキ：そうなんですよ！　メーカーはどうして、そんなに安くできるんですか？

小浜：安くなるには理由があるからね。どんな理由だと思う？

マキ：メーカー間の競争が激しいからじゃないですか？　量販店には、いろいろなメーカーの液晶テレビが、ずらっと並んでいましたもの。

小浜：ああ、それも1つの理由なんだけど、意外や意外、前に話した「固定費」が、この安値に関係している。中でも、液晶テレビを作るための工場建設にかかる費用、つまり**設備投資**が、低価格と関係あるんだよ。

マキ：設備投資と製品価格のつながりなんて、考えたことありません。

小浜：じゃあまず、企業がどうやって設備投資を回収するのか考えてみよう。

マキ：そりゃあ、設備投資をした分、製品の価格をちょっと上げるんですよ。

小浜：その通り！　でも、設備投資の費用を製品価格に上乗せするとしても、製品1つに対する上乗せ分はできるだけ抑えたいものだよね。それにはどうしたらいいと思う？

Maki: Well, the cost to be added to the product price can be calculated by dividing the total investment by the production quantity of the product. Therefore, if they increase the production quantity, the investment can be divided among more units. So, the manufacturer produces in large quantities to lower the capital investment cost per unit of the product!

Obama: That's right. If the supply increases, the price will decrease accordingly. That's why the price of LCD television sets has been falling. Furthermore, the competition is very severe, as you mentioned earlier, so all manufacturers are very eager to lower their unit price.

Maki: So, in theory, they will all be increasing their production quantity to lower their unit price.

Obama: That's right. From each manufacturer's narrow viewpoint, they decide upon a reasonable production quantity, but all manufacturers are now in the process of increasing the production quantity. This results in a state of over-production and over-supply, which will lower the price further.

Maki: So, the sales and cost plan made at the start of production will be derailed.

Prof. Obama: It sometimes happens that each individual's rational action does not lead to rational results overall. We call this the "fallacy of composition".

Keywords

生産過剰
over-production

商品の生産量が、消費を上回っている状態を指す。市場に出しても商品が売れないため、在庫の増加や値下がりが生じる。

供給過剰
over-supply

需要と供給のバランスがとれておらず、商品の市場への供給量が需要を上回っている状態を指す。商品があふれて売れ残りが発生するため、その解消のため、値崩れが生じやすい。
＝生産過剰

合成の誤謬
fallacy of composition

経済学の用語で、ミクロの視点では正しいことであっても、それらが合成されたマクロの世界では必ずしも、意図した最適の結果が生じるわけではないことを指す。

マキ：うーん、製品価格への上乗せ額は、設備投資の総額を製品の生産数で割れば出せるから、生産数を増やせば、設備投資額をより多くの数で割ることができる。つまり、メーカーは、製品1個当たりの設備投資コストを抑えるため、大量に生産する！

小浜：その通り。そして供給が増加すれば、それに応じて価格は低下する。だから、液晶テレビの価格はどんどん下がっているわけさ。それに加えて、さっき言っていた競争の激しさがあるから、メーカーはどこも1台当たりの価格を下げようと躍起になる。

マキ：だから理論上、生産量を増やして1台の価格を抑えようとするんですね。

小浜：そうなんだ。メーカー個別のミクロな視点では合理的に生産量を決定しているのに、それがメーカー全体のマクロでは、どんどん生産量を増やし続ける事態を招いているってことだ。その結果、生産過剰、供給過剰を引き起こして、価格がさらに下落してしまう。

マキ：それじゃ、生産を開始する時に立てた売上高やコストの計画が狂っちゃうじゃないですか。

小浜：個々としては合理的な行動をしているのに、全体として見た場合に、その個々の行動の結果が最適にはならないことがある。これが、「合成の誤謬」と呼ばれるものだ。

Words & Phrases   ①②③……は、その語が登場した行数を表しています。

① LCD　液晶ディスプレー。Liquid Crystal Displayの略
② get ready for　～に備える
② terrestrial digital television broadcasting　地上波デジタルテレビ放送
⑥ manufacturer　製造業者、メーカー
⑥ cope with　～に耐える、立ち向かう
⑩ cutthroat　非情な、生きるか死ぬかの
⑳ recover　取り戻す、回収する
㉗ calculate　計算する、算出する
㉘ divide　割る
㉘ quantity　数量⇔quality 質
㊵ narrow　狭い
㊻ derail　外れる、横道にそれる
㊼ rational　合理的な

Chapter 5

35 減価償却のマジック

Maki: There's one thing I've been wondering, what exactly is depreciation?

Prof. Obama: Oh, I haven't explained it in detail yet. In capital investment, the decreasing value of things such as factories and machinery that have a limited service life needs to be taken into account. Depreciation is accounted for as a cost for each period during which the value of its assets is being used.

Maki: As a cost?

Obama: Yes. Suppose there is an investment of 100 billion yen to purchase factories and machinery that are to be used for a period of 20 years. In this case, we divide 100 billion by 20 years, and the depreciation each year will be five billion yen. But suppose that the whole 100 billion yen is taken as an expense at one time. Then, that year's account will be hugely in the red. On the other hand, profits in subsequent years will be huge. The idea of adjusting these inequalities is called depreciation.

Maki: In other words, cash flow is generated at the time of capital investment, but in accounting, it's treated as depreciation—it's listed as an expense by dividing the investment by the number of years it's expected to be used for. So, depreciation is one of the "expenses that do not cause cash-outs"!

Obama: Correct! So, the depreciation every year is an expense which is generated regardless of the production quantity; that is, it is an item in the fixed costs. Incidentally, such items as depreciation, for which the cost is decided based on past decisions, are called "committed costs".

KEYWORDS

減価償却
depreciation

使用することによって年々消耗する固定資産の「価値の減る分（減価）」を、企業が経費として計上すること。定額法と定率法があるが、いずれも実際にお金が流出するわけではない。

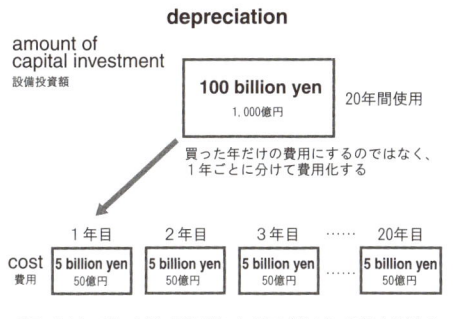

depreciation

amount of
capital investment
設備投資額

100 billion yen
1,000億円　　20年間使用

買った年だけの費用にするのではなく、
1年ごとに分けて費用化する

	1年目	2年目	3年目	……	20年目
cost 費用	5 billion yen 50億円	5 billion yen 50億円	5 billion yen 50億円		5 billion yen 50億円

＊費用の分け方には上のような定額法以外にも、当初の償却の多い定率法などがある。

耐用年数
service life

固定資産が企業で事業に使用されてから、少しずつ価値が減少していき、ついには役に立たなくなるまでの期間のこと。period of depreciation や durable years と呼ばれることもある。

コミティッドコスト
committed costs

commit は「約束する」なので、「約束された費用、決定済み費用」という意味。過去になされた投資などの意思決定により、その後の一定期間に必ず発生するコストを指す。

TRANSLATION

マキ：気になっていたんですけど、減価償却って、どういうことですか？

小浜教授：そうか、まだ詳しく説明してなかったね。設備投資のうち、工場や機械のように耐用年数に限りのあるものについては、価値の減少を計上していく必要があるんだ。そして減価償却とは、資産の価値を、使用期間に応じて「費用化」することなんだ。

マキ：費用化ですか？

小浜：ああ。1000億円の設備投資で工場や機械を購入して、それらを20年間使用するとしよう。この場合、1000億円÷20年で、1年ごとの減価償却費は50億円になる。だが仮にその1000億円全額を費用として一時に計上すると、その年は大赤字になり、その一方で、その次の年からは黒字が増えてしまう。このでこぼこを調整する考え方が、減価償却なんだ。

マキ：要するに、キャッシュフローは設備投資の時に発生しているけど、会計上はそれを、減価償却費として、投資額をその設備が使用されると期待される年数で分割して費用として計上する。つまり、減価償却費も「お金の出ていかない費用」の1つなんですね！

小浜：その通り！　だから毎年の減価償却費は、生産量に関係なく毎年発生してしまう費用、つまり固定費の仲間なんだ。ついでに言うと、この減価償却費のように、過去の意思決定で、その後のコストが決まってしまうものを「コミティッドコスト」という。

Maki: So what happens if a machine is still being operated normally after the depreciation period ends?

Obama: Good question! After the depreciation period ends, the fixed cost of depreciation that was added to the product price will disappear. That's all.

Maki: One of the fixed costs disappears! In other words, the production cost goes down. So, if they continue to sell the product, the profit will increase, won't it?

Obama: Yes, as a matter of fact, here's another reason why the price of LCD TV's has been falling. Suppose there's a depreciation of 10,000 yen per set, and the capital investment was 100 billion yen. After the production of 10 million sets, the depreciation comes to an end. If the machinery can still be used after producing 10 million sets, there is no depreciation for the sets produced afterwards. Naturally, the profit rate will greatly increase.

Maki: I see. They want to sell a certain number of products as soon as possible so that the depreciation can come to an early end. They want to finish depreciation as quickly as they can, to allow them to start selling the products with a higher profit sooner. For that purpose, they may lower the price a little bit, which makes the price of LCD TV's lower!

Obama: Yes, this is the magic of fixed cost depreciation.

KEYWORDS

固定費償却後は大幅利益アップ

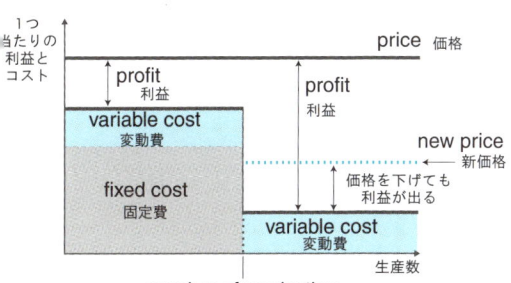

1つ当たりの利益とコスト
- price 価格
- profit 利益
- variable cost 変動費
- fixed cost 固定費
- new price 新価格
- 価格を下げても利益が出る
- variable cost 変動費
- number of production to pay off fixed cost 固定費を償却する生産数
- 生産数

マキ：じゃあ、減価償却の期間を過ぎてもまだ正常に動く場合は、どうなるんですか？

小浜：いい質問だ。減価償却の期間が終了したら、それまで製品価格に転嫁されていた減価償却費という固定費がなくなる、ただそれだけだ。

マキ：固定費の1つがなくなる！ つまり、製造費用が減るんですよね。じゃあ、それまで通り製品を売り続けたら、利益だけ増えるんじゃないですか？

小浜：そう、実はここにも、液晶テレビの価格がどんどん下がっている理由があるんだ。液晶テレビ1台当たり1万円の償却負担がかかっているとしよう。設備投資が1000億円だとすると、1000万台生産すれば、減価償却は終了ということになる。1000万台生産した後も設備がまだ使用可能だったら、それ以降に生産するテレビは、償却負担がゼロ。当然、利益率は大幅にアップする。

マキ：なるほど。償却負担が早く終わるよう、一定数の製品をできる限り早く売りたい。早く償却を終えて、利益率の高い製品を少しでも早く売り出せるようにしよう。そのためには、少しくらい売値を安くすることもある。だからまた、液晶テレビは安くなる、ってことですね！

小浜：そう、これが固定費償却のマジックなんだ。

Words & Phrases   ①②③……は、その語が登場した行数を表しています。

- ③ in detail　詳細に
- ⑤ take ~ into account　~を計算に入れる
- ⑨ Suppose ~　仮に~だとしてみよう
- ⑩ purchase　購入する
- ⑯ inequality　不公平、不平等
- ㉓ regardless of ~　~にかかわらず
- ㉔ incidentally　ちなみに
- ㉗ operate　運転する、操作する
- ㉛ disappear　消失する、姿を消す
- ㊴ comes to an end　終わる

Chapter 5

36日目 ダンピングと、日本の固定費処理

TR12

Maki: It seems to me that the accounting figures vary depending on the accounting method, such as using a shorter depreciation period, as well as on things such as the difference between production costs and costs of sales.

Prof. Obama: In particular, accounting for fixed cost depreciation can be quite troublesome. Have you heard the term "dumping", Maki?

Maki: I remember learning that the United States sued Japan, saying that Japan was selling steel products too cheaply and that higher customs duties should be introduced to stop their dumping.

Obama: Yes, that's it. Dumping in the Japanese language translates as "unreasonably low prices", and it means selling at less than cost. It's a good example of the magic of fixed cost depreciation.

Maki: Was it really necessary to export the products at a price lower than cost and sell them abroad?

Obama: No, not really.

Maki: No? Then, why were they sold so cheaply?

Obama: Well, let's think about it. How could they sell the products so cheaply?

Maki: They'd need to hold down the manufacturing cost by purchasing the materials cheaply or by cutting the personnel and transportation expenses.

Obama: That's right, but when they export something, there will be an import duty on it in foreign countries, causing extra ex-

KEYWORDS

関税
customs duties
貨物が国境などの経済的境界を通過するときに課せられる租税。一般に、外国からの輸入品に課す import duties（輸入税）を指す。国内産業の保護と租税収入を目的とする。

不当廉価
unreasonably low prices
原価を無視した、利益が上がらないほどの安値（で販売すること）。原価割れで販売すること。

製造コスト
manufacturing cost
商品を製造するのにかかった費用のこと。原材料費や人件費などが含まれるが、宣伝や販売にかかる費用は含まれない。

輸入税
import duty
関税のうち、外から中へ貨物が持ち込まれるときに課せられる租税。

TRANSLATION

マキ：減価償却期間を短くするといった会計上の処理の仕方とか、製造原価と売上原価に違いがあるとかで、数字って随分、変わってしまうみたいですね。

小浜教授：中でも固定費の償却の会計処理は、なかなか厄介なんだ。マキさん、「ダンピング」って言葉を聞いたことあるかい？

マキ：日本が売っている鉄製品は価格が安すぎる。ダンピングを阻止するために関税を高くしろ、とアメリカが日本を訴えたことがあるって習ったような気がします。

小浜：そう、それだ。ダンピングは日本語では不当廉価と呼ばれて、いわゆる原価割れ販売のことなんだが、これも固定費償却マジックのいい例なんだ。

マキ：コスト割れしてまで、製品をわざわざ輸出して外国で売る必要があったんですか？

小浜：いや、ないね。

マキ：ええ？ じゃあどうして安売りが行われたんですか？

小浜：いいかい、ちょっと考えてみよう。どうしたら製品をうんと安く販売できるだろうか？

マキ：材料を安く仕入れたり、人件費や輸送費などを切り詰めたりして、製造コストをできるだけ抑える必要があります。

小浜：そうなんだけど、何かを輸出すると、海外ではそれに輸入税がかかったりして、国内で販売するときよりも多くの

penses compared with selling in Japan. So, it's necessary to lower the price to offset those extra expenses. Therefore, they turned their attention to the handling of fixed costs.

Maki: What do you mean?

Obama: They didn't transfer the fixed cost for production to the exported products; they only transferred it to the products for the domestic market. So, Japan claimed that they were "not selling the products at a price lower than cost; therefore, it was not dumping".

Maki: Is that so? Isn't that devious? The Americans must have felt that Japan were selling the products cheaply by deception.

Obama: The American argument was that the fixed cost should be transferred evenly to all the products regardless of whether the products were for domestic use or for export. That's why the U.S. sued Japan for dumping. As it was related to the steel industry, which was quite important to the U.S., the Americans were quite sensitive. In fact, Japan and the U.S. had a long argument about it.

Maki: So, the way you choose to handle fixed costs can cause real trouble. But, Professor Obama, can we do this kind of thing in accounting so easily?

Obama: Well, let's take a look at that now, by looking at an income statement.

KEYWORDS

損益計算書
income statement
☞ 2日目

費用がかかる。だから、余分な費用の分だけ、価格をもっと安くしなくちゃいけない。そこで、固定費の処理に着目したんだ。

マキ：どういうことですか？

小浜：生産にかかる固定費を輸出分には転嫁しないで、国内市場向けの製品だけに負担させたんだ。だから日本側の言い分としては「コスト割れして売っているわけじゃないから、ダンピングには当たりません」となるわけ。

マキ：えーっ、でもそんなの屁理屈じゃないですか？　アメリカからしたら、日本がズルして安く売りつけているような感じですよ。

小浜：国内向けであろうと海外向けであろうと、製品にはすべて均等に固定費を負担させるべきというのがアメリカの主張。だからアメリカは、日本をダンピング提訴したんだ。もっとも、鉄というアメリカにとって重要な産業にかかわる話だったからこそ、アメリカが非常に神経質になった面もあるけどね。実際に日本とアメリカは、その後、このことで随分ともめたんだ。

マキ：やっぱり、固定費の処理って本当に問題ですね。でも先生、こういうことは会計上簡単にできちゃうものなんですか？

小浜：じゃあ今度は実際にそれを、**損益計算書**を見ながら考えていこう！

Words & Phrases

①②③……は、その語が登場した行数を表しています。

- ① accounting　会計（処理）
- ① vary　変化する、異なるものになる
- ⑥ troublesome　厄介な
- ⑥ dumping　ダンピング、不当に価格を下げること
- ⑧ sue　訴える
- ⑫ translate　訳せる
- ㉒ hold down　引き下げる
- ㉓ personnel expense　人件費
- ㉔ transportation expense　輸送費
- ㉘ offset　相殺する、埋め合わせをする
- ㉙ handling　処理、対処
- ㉝ domestic　自国の、国内向けの
- ㉝ claim　主張する
- ㊱ devious　不正な、ごまかした
- ㊲ deception　騙し、いかさま
- ㊳ argument　論拠、討論
- ㊴ evenly　同じように

Chapter 5

37日目 財務・管理・税務の３つの会計

Prof. Obama: First, let's review what we've learned. Do you remember how "net income" is calculated in an income statement?

Maki: Well, starting with "net sales", we deduct "cost of sales", "selling and general administrative expenses", "non-operating profit and loss", and "special gains and losses" one by one, and that gives us "net income".

Obama: Correct! This way of calculating an income statement is called "full costing". Did you notice something about the handling of "fixed costs"?

Maki: Oh, fixed costs? Just a second … Fixed costs are a part of the "cost of production", aren't they? Oh, I see. We've only deducted cost of sales, which means that we've only considered the fixed costs for the products that are actually sold.

Obama: Exactly! That is a characteristic of full costing, and also a characteristic of the handling of fixed costs in financial accounting.

Maki: Just a moment, Professor Obama. What do you mean by "financial accounting"?

Obama: Financial accounting is accounting that's done to prepare financial statements that are to be disclosed to the public. There are many kinds of accounting, but business people need to remember three kinds: "Financial Accounting", "managerial accounting" and "tax accounting".

Maki: How are they different?

Obama: As I just said, financial accounting is for financial statements going outside the company. It's based on specified legal

KEYWORDS

当期純利益
net income

売上高ー売上原価ー販管費ー営業外損益ー特別損益＝当期純利益

☞ 11日目

全部原価計算
full costing

変動費と固定費を区別せず、固定費の配賦基準に沿って配分処理されたすべての費用を製品に反映させて原価を計算する方法。一般に原価計算といった場合は、この全部原価計算を指す。

財務会計
financial accounting

株主や金融機関、税務当局などの外部の利害関係者に、財務諸表を用いて報告することを目的とした会計。

管理会計
managerial accounting

財務会計上では報告を求められていない、社内的な経営状態の把握と分析、その結果に基づく改善活動に役立つ情報（例えば、製品別売上高、原価、限界利益など）を得るための会計。企業では通常、前項の財務会計と併せて運用される。

税務会計
tax accounting

所得や税額など、納税当局への申告を目的とした会計の総称。

TRANSLATION

小浜教授：さて、まずは復習から。損益計算書における「当期純利益」はどのように計算されるんだったかな？

マキ：えーと、「売上高」から「売上原価」「販売費及び一般管理費」「営業外損益」「特別損益」などを順番に控除して「当期純利益」を算出します。

小浜：正解。損益計算書を作る上でのベースになっているこの計算方法が、「全部原価計算」という考え方なんだ。「固定費」の扱いについて何か気付いたかい？

マキ：え、固定費ですか？　ちょっと待ってください。固定費ってことは「製造原価」の一部ですよね。あ、分かった。売上原価しか控除していないってことは、売れた製品の分の固定費しか考えられていないんだ！

小浜：その通り！　それが全部原価計算の特徴であり、財務会計上の固定費の扱い方の特徴でもあるんだよ。

マキ：ちょっと待ってください、先生。「財務会計」上ってどういう意味ですか？

小浜：財務会計は、一般に向けて公開する財務諸表を作成するための会計のこと。ちなみに会計にはたくさんの種類があるんだけど、ビジネスマンが覚えておかなくちゃいけないのは、「財務会計」と「管理会計」、それに「税務会計」の3つだ。

マキ：それぞれ、どう違うんですか？

小浜：今言ったように、財務会計は、社外向けの財務諸表用のもので、定められた基準に基づいて、財務状態や経営成績やキャッシュフローの状況を報告するんだ。

standards, and it reports the financial conditions, management results and cash flow of a company.

Maki: By "outside the company", do you mean to consumers and shareholders, like us?

Obama: Right. To creditors and shareholders. Managerial accounting, on the other hand, is accounting that measures performance within the company. Its purpose is to provide the information required to run a company. The last kind of accounting, tax accounting, is accounting to calculate tax. But, in relation to the handling of fixed costs, we only need to look at financial accounting and managerial accounting. So, to return to "full costing", which is the calculation method of fixed costs in financial accounting, tell me about fixed costs again.

Maki: We only calculate the cost of the products that are actually sold, and the fixed costs that have been used for the unsold products are not taken into account.

Obama: Yes, the unsold products become inventory, and they are listed as stock in the assets column of the balance sheet. So, in full costing, it sometimes happens that the profit may appear to be larger than it actually is because high production has increased the stock.

Maki: Well, then, the information in an income statement may give people a misleading impression. Managers and executives might abuse this mechanism.

Obama: You're right. But, people are resourceful. If there are any defects in a system, people usually improve them. There is an idea called "direct costing", which has improved the defects of full costing.

KEYWORDS

棚卸資産
inventory

原材料や製品、商品、半製品、仕掛品といった、企業が、将来の生産活動や販売活動のために保有する資産。いわゆる「在庫」。

☞ 10日目

在庫
stock

会計上で「棚卸資産」と呼ばれるものの通称。

直接原価計算
direct costing

製品原価を計算する際に、変動費と固定費を区別し、変動費のみを製品に反映させて原価を計算し、固定費は期間費用として処理する計算方法。変動費と固定費を区別する点において斬新で、損益分岐点の考え方の基礎となる概念だが、財務会計上で認められていないことから、実務では全部原価計算を用いる場合がほとんど。

マキ：社外にというのは、私たちのような消費者や株主にってことかですか？

小浜：その通り。与信者と投資家にだね。それに対して管理会計は、企業内のパフォーマンスを把握するための会計のこと。会社の経営を行っていくために必要な情報を提供するのが、管理会計の目的だ。最後の税務会計は、税金を計算するための会計のことだが、固定費の扱いに関しては、財務会計と管理会計の２つに注目すればいい。それじゃあ、財務会計における固定費の計算方法である「全部原価計算」に話を戻すために、もう一度、固定費について説明してごらん。

マキ：売れた分の原価だけを計算して、売れ残りの製品にも発生したはずの固定費は計算されないんですよね。

小浜：ああ、売れ残った製品は**棚卸資産**になり、貸借対照表の資産の部に**在庫**として計上されるんだ。だから、全部原価計算では、たくさん作って在庫を増やした方が、（帳簿上の）利益が実際よりも大きくなることがあるんだ。

マキ：それじゃあ、損益計算書の情報は人々に誤解を招く印象を与えてしまうかもしれませんね。経営陣がこの仕組みを悪用しないとも限らないですし。

小浜：そうなんだ。しかし、人間というのは、システムに欠陥があるとそれを改善するところがすごい。全部原価計算の欠点を改善した「**直接原価計算**」という考えもあるんだよ。

Words & Phrases

①②③……は、その語が登場した行数を表しています。

① review　復習する、おさらいする
③ deduct　控除する、差し引く
⑭ characteristic　特徴、特質
⑳ disclose　開示する、公開する
㉖ specified　規定の、特定の
㉖ legal　法律上の
㉛ creditor　債権者、与信者
㊷ take into account ～　～を考慮する、配慮する
㊾ misleading　誤解を招く恐れのある
㊿ abuse　悪用する
(51) resourceful　頭がいい、優れている
(52) defect　欠陥、不備、短所

Chapter 5

38 直接原価計算をしてみよう！

Prof. Obama: Now let's continue. We were studying direct costing, weren't we? What do you think it is?

Maki: Well, since "full costing" is the method for financial accounting, is "direct costing" what we use for managerial accounting?

Obama: Exactly! Let's have a look at the calculations it involves. To obtain net income in direct costing, first, we subtract the variable costs from net sales. From the result, which is called marginal profit or contribution profit, we subtract "all" the fixed costs. This avoids the fixed costs being included in the stock.

Maki: That means that all the costs, not only for the goods sold, but also for the goods manufactured, are recorded as either profits or losses. Hmm, I think I understand.

Obama: Well, let's go through an example. Suppose company A's fixed costs for their factory are 100 million yen and the variable cost for one product is 5,000 yen. Now, let's calculate the cost for this product if company A makes 10,000 pieces in a year. First, how about the cost in the case of full costing?

Maki: Well, to work out the fixed cost of one product, we divide 100 million yen by 10,000 pieces, which equals 10,000 yen. The variable cost is 5,000 yen, so the fixed cost is 15,000 yen in all.

Obama: Correct. Then, suppose company A makes 100,000 pieces of the same product in a year?

Maki: If we divide 100 million yen by 100,000 pieces, we get the fixed cost of one product, which is 1,000 yen. By adding the variable cost of 5,000 yen, we get a new cost of 6,000 yen.

Obama: It's simple up to this point. Now, suppose the price of this

KEYWORDS

直接原価計算
direct costing
☞ 37 日目

全部原価計算
full costing
☞ 37 日目

限界利益／貢献利益
marginal profit / contribution profit
売上高から変動費を控除した利益のこと。限界利益は、管理会計の概念の1つ。限界利益には固定費が含まれる。固定費の回収に"貢献する"ことに注目した言い方が貢献利益。

在庫
stock
☞ 37 日目

TRANSLATION

小浜教授：さあ、続けようか。直接原価計算についてだったね。直接原価計算とは何だろうか？

マキ：ええと、「全部原価計算」が財務会計の計算方法だったから……もしかして、「直接原価計算」は管理会計上で用いるものですか？

小浜：その通り！　早速、用いられる計算方法を見てみよう。直接原価計算で当期純利益を求めるには、まず、売上高から変動費を引く。限界利益とか貢献利益と呼ばれるこの値から、今度は固定費を"全額"引く。これで、固定費が在庫として計上されることを回避しているんだ。

マキ：売った分だけでなく、製造した分にかかった費用がすべて損益に組み込まれるんですね。分かった気がします。

小浜：それじゃ、例を挙げて計算してみよう。A社では製造現場で固定費が1億円かかり、製品1つ当たりの変動費が5000円だとする。じゃあ、A社がこの製品を1年間で1万個作ったときの原価を計算しようか。まず、全部原価計算で行った場合は？

マキ：えーっと、製品1つ当たりの原価を出すには、製品1つ当たりの固定費が1億円÷1万個の1万円で、それに変動費が5000円だから、合わせて1万5000円です。

小浜：そうだ。じゃあ、A社がこの同じ製品を1年間に10万個作ったとすれば？

マキ：製品1つ当たりの固定費が1億円÷10万個の1000円に減るから、変動費の5000円を足しても、原価は6000円に減りますね。

小浜：ここまでは簡単。じゃあ、この製

product is 20,000 yen. Which would be more profitable, 10,000 or 100,000 pieces?

Maki: Well, the profit per product is "the price minus the cost". So, in the case of making 10,000 pieces, 20,000 yen minus 15,000 yen makes a profit of 5,000 yen per unit. While in the case of making 100,000 pieces, 200,000 yen minus 6,000 yen makes a profit of 14,000 yen per unit. Apparently, it is more profitable to make 100,000 pieces. But, let me see. It's not always the case that 100,000 pieces can be sold. It may be that a lot of them remain unsold.

Obama: That's the point.

全部原価計算と在庫

変動費（1個あたり）5千円、
固定費（年間）1億円の場合も……

	1万個生産の場合	10万個生産の場合
売上高	200 百万円	200 百万円
売上原価	150	60
売上総利益	50	140

↓

多く作った方が利益が大きい！！

……………… しかし ………………

在庫	0円	540百万円
		（6,000×9万個）

↓

固定費の一部（9千万円）が在庫に含まれる！

KEYWORDS

品の売価が2万円だとすると、1万個と、10万個とでは、どちら（を作った方）が儲かるでしょう？

マキ：えーと、1つ当たりの儲けは「売価−原価」だから、1万個作ったときは2万−1万5000円で1個当たり5000円。10万個作ったときは、2万−6000円で1個当たり1万4000円。断然、10万個の方が儲かりますね！　あれ、でも待てよ。必ずしも10万個全部が売れるわけではなくて、もしかしたら、たくさん売れ残っちゃうかもしれませんよね。

小浜：そう、そこがポイントさ！

Words & Phrases

①②③……は、その語が登場した行数を表しています。

⑤ involve　用いる、導入する
⑨ avoid　回避する、逃れる
⑬ go through　検討する
⑱ work out　解く、算出する
㉗ profitable　利益になる、儲かる

Chapter 5

39 2種類の原価計算方法と利益の意味

Prof. Obama: Suppose the supply and demand of this product can be balanced at product sales of 10,000 pieces, but only 10,000 of the 100,000 pieces are sold. In this case, if it is in full costing …

Maki: The unsold products are listed as assets. So, even if 90,000 pieces are unsold out of the 100,000 pieces made, the profit on the books may not be affected. But, the unsold 90,000 pieces remain as inventory …

Obama: Well, let's consider the case of direct costing. In this case, whether 10,000 pieces or 100,000 pieces are made, the variable cost is 5,000 yen times 10,000 pieces sold, which equals 50 million yen. And the sales amount, which is the selling price of 20,000 yen times 10,000 pieces, is 200 million yen regardless of the quantity made. Therefore, the marginal profit is 200 million minus 50 million, which is 150 million yen. From this amount, the fixed cost of 100 million yen is deducted, leaving 50 million yen as profit. If we divide the profit by the quantity sold, 10,000 pieces, we can obtain a profit of 5,000 yen per piece. In other words, direct costing shows us the profit that is not affected by the quantity made.

Maki: I see. But, why don't we use the direct costing method when we make an income statement?

Obama: There's a good reason for not using direct costing. An income statement is made to be disclosed to the public, you know. If we first list all of the costs, using direct costing, then a big loss will be shown. On the other hand, when the products with costs already allocated are sold, a big profit will be shown.

Keywords

需要と供給
supply and demand

物品などの財を買い求めようとする欲求が需要。一方の供給は、財やサービスを提供する経済活動のこと。自由競争市場では、両者のバランスで市場価格や需給量が調整され、決定される。

直接原価計算

	1万個生産の場合	10万個生産の場合
売上高	200 百万円	200 百万円
－変動費	50	50
限界利益	150	150
－固定費	100	100
利益	50	50

すべての固定費を引く

生産量にかかわらず利益は一定

在庫	0円	450百万円 （5千円×9万個）

Translation

小浜教授：仮に、この製品の需要と供給のバランスが取れる点が1万個で、1万個きっちりしか売れないとする。このとき、全部原価計算だったら……。

マキ：売れ残りは資産として計上されるから、仮に10万個作って9万個が売れ残ったとしても、表向きの利益に影響は出ない。でも、9万個の売れ残りが、在庫資産として残るから……。

小浜：じゃあ、直接原価計算の場合を考えよう。この場合、1万個作ろうと10万個作ろうと、変動費は売れた1万個分の5000万円。そして売上高も、2万円×1万個だから、作った数にかかわりなく2億円。だから限界利益は、2億円－5000万円の1億5000万円だ。その額から固定費の1億円を引くと5000万円が利益として残る。この利益を売れた個数の1万で割ると、1個当たりの利益、5000円が得られる。つまりこの直接原価生産は、どれだけ作ったかに影響されないで利益を把握することができるんだ。

マキ：なるほど。なのにどうして、損益計算書を作るときにも、直接原価計算を使うようにしないんですか？

小浜：それにはちゃんとした理由があるんだ。損益計算書は、一般に公開することを目的としているよね。そのとき、直接原価計算の方法で費用だけを先に計上すると、マイナスだけが大きく出てしまう。一方で、先に費用計上だけがなされた製品が後で売れると、今度

When we look at the income statement using this method, we cannot compare the cost that has actually been generated to a certain sales amount. Therefore, in financial accounting, we try to list both the sales amount of the certain period and the costs of it at the same time.

Maki: In other words, financial accounting and managerial accounting are for different purposes, and we use full costing or direct costing, depending on the purpose.

Obama: Right, I think you understand it all pretty well. What this all shows us is that profit is only a concept in accounting.

Maki: It's true. I was surprised to learn that the profit changes depending on the calculation method you use.

Obama: We've talked about a difficult topic, but the important thing to remember is that we need to be flexible so that we can look at things from various angles.

直接原価計算

KEYWORDS

　　は利益のみが大きく出る。これでは、損益計算書を見た時に、売上げに対してどれだけの費用が発生しているのかという比較ができないんだ。だから財務会計では、売上高の計上と費用の計上の時期をできるだけ一致させようとするんだ。

マキ：つまり、財務会計と管理会計は目的が違うものだから、目的に応じて全部原価計算と直接原価計算を使いわけるってことですね。

小浜：そういうこと。今までの説明を聞いて十分に分かったかと思うけど、利益というのは結局のところ、会計上の概念でしかないんだ。

マキ：確かに、計算方法を変えるだけで利益額まで変わるなんて、驚きました。

小浜：随分難しい話になってしまったけど、何事もいろいろな角度から見れるように、頭を柔らかくしていかなくてはいけないね。

Words & Phrases　①②③……は、その語が登場した行数を表しています。

② balance　均衡をとる、勘定があう
⑫ regardless of　～にかかわらず
㉖ allocate　配分する
㊵ flexible　柔軟に対応できる

Chapter 5

REVIEW EXERCISE
Chapter 5 で学んだ内容を復習しよう

TR16 まずは、チャンツのリズムに乗せて Keywords を発音しましょう。

- ☐ **capital investment**
  設備投資
- ☐ **over-production**
  生産過剰
- ☐ **over-supply**
  供給過剰
- ☐ **fallacy of composition**
  合成の誤謬
- ☐ **depreciation**
  減価償却
- ☐ **service life**
  耐用年数
- ☐ **committed costs**
  コミティッドコスト
- ☐ **customs duties**
  関税

< pause >

- ☐ **manufacturing cost**
  製造コスト
- ☐ **import duty**
  輸入税
- ☐ **income statement**
  損益計算書
- ☐ **full costing**
  全部原価計算
- ☐ **financial accounting**
  財務会計
- ☐ **managerial accounting**
  管理会計
- ☐ **tax accounting**
  税務会計
- ☐ **direct costing**
  直接原価計算

< pause >

- ☐ **contribution**
  貢献
- ☐ **supply and demand**
  需要と供給
- ☐ **manufacturer**
  製造業者、メーカー
- ☐ **rational**
  合理的な
- ☐ **inequality**
  不公平、不平等
- ☐ **dumping**
  ダンピング
- ☐ **transportation expense**
  輸送費
- ☐ **offset**
  相殺する、埋め合わせる

< pause >

- ☐ **domestic**
  国内向けの、自国の
- ☐ **deception**
  騙し、いかさま
- ☐ **deduct**
  控除する、差し引く
- ☐ **disclose**
  公開する、開示する
- ☐ **creditor**
  債権者
- ☐ **devious**
  不正な、ごまかした
- ☐ **defect**
  欠陥、不備、短所
- ☐ **allocate**
  配分する

会社の実力を英語で診断！

以下の指示に従い、全部原価計算と、直接原価計算を、自分でやってみましょう。

問 下記の条件で、商品を1万個製造した場合と10万個製造した場合について、「全部原価計算」による損益計算書と、「直接原価計算」による損益計算書を作って、以下に記入してください。どちらも、1万個販売するものとします。なお、（　）の空欄も併せて記入してください。

条件：販売価格：1個あたり20円
　　　変動製造原価：1個あたり5円
　　　固定製造原価：50,000円
　　　変動販売費：1個あたり3円
　　　固定販売費及び一般管理費：30,000円

ケース1

（10,000個作り、10,000個すべてを販売した場合）

Statement of income by full costing metod

Net sales		( )
Cost of sales		
Opening balance of finished goods	0	
Cost of finished goods manufactured	( )	
Sub total	( )	
Closing balance of finished goods	( )	
Net cost of sales		( )
Gross profit		( )
Selling and general administrative expenses		( )
( )		( )

ケース2

（100,000個作り、10,000個を販売、90,000個は在庫として売れ残った場合）

Statement of income by full costing metod

Net sales		( )
Cost of sales		
Opening balance of finished goods	0	
Cost of finished goods manufactured	( )	
Sub total	( )	
Closing balance of finished goods	( )	
Net cost of sales		( )
Gross profit		( )
Selling and general administrative expenses		( )
( )		( )

（10,000個作り、10,000個すべてを販売した場合）

Statement of income by direct costing metod

Net sales		( )
Variable manufacturing costs	( )	
Variable selling expenses	( )	
Sub total of variable costs and expenses		( )
(Marginal profit, (Contribution profit))		( )
Fixed manufacturing costs	( )	
Fixed selling and general administrative expenses	( )	
Sub total of fixed costs and expenses		( )
( )		( )

（100,000個作り、10,000個を販売、90,000個は在庫として売れ残った場合）

Statement of income by direct costing metod

Net sales		( )
Variable manufacturing costs	( )	
Variable selling expenses	( )	
Sub total of variable costs and expenses		( )
(Marginal profit, (Contribution profit))		( )
Fixed manufacturing costs	( )	
Fixed selling and general administrative expenses	( )	
Sub total of fixed costs and expenses		( )
( )		( )

解答と解説

ケース1
（10,000個作り、10,000個すべてを販売した場合）

全部原価計算による損益計算書

売上高		200,000
売上原価		
期首製品棚卸高	0	
当期製品製造原価	100,000	
小計	100,000	
期末製品棚卸高	0	
売上原価　小計		100,000
売上総利益		100,000
販売費及び一般管理費		60,000
営業利益		40,000

直接原価計算による損益計算書

売上高		200,000
変動製造原価	50,000	
変動販売費	30,000	
変動費 小計		80,000
限界利益（貢献利益）		120,000
固定製造原価	50,000	
固定販売費及び一般管理費	30,000	
固定費 小計		80,000
営業利益		40,000

ケース2
（100,000個作り、10,000個を販売、90,000個は在庫として売れ残った場合）

全部原価計算による損益計算書

売上高		200,000
売上原価		
期首製品棚卸高	0	
当期製品製造原価	550,000	
小計	550,000	
期末製品棚卸高	495,000	
売上原価　小計		55,000
売上総利益		145,000
販売費及び一般管理費		60,000
営業利益		85,000

直接原価計算による損益計算書

売上高		200,000
変動製造原価	50,000	
変動販売費	30,000	
変動費 小計		80,000
限界利益（貢献利益）		120,000
固定製造原価	50,000	
固定販売費及び一般管理費	30,000	
固定費 小計		80,000
営業利益		40,000

【解説】全部計算では、固定製造原価50,000円も加えた原価の総額（550,000円）を、製造した個数10万で割るので、1個あたりの製造原価は5.5円。在庫が9万個なので、期末製品棚卸額は495,000円となる。

Chapter 5 のまとめ

直接原価計算（direct costing）とは？
　全部原価計算の欠点を克服し、企業のパフォーマンスを正しく把握することを目指して開発された「管理会計」上の概念

直接原価計算（direct costing）
　固定費が在庫に資産として計上されない原価の計算方法。売れた数によらず、製造にかかった固定費のすべてを期間内の費用として差し引いてしまうため、売れなかった分の製造コストが資産に残ることはない。

■**直接原価計算**
　　売上高 net sales
　－変動費 variable costs
　　限界利益 marginal profit
　－固定費 fixed costs
　　利益 net profit

全部原価計算 full costing
　財務会計で求められている原価の計算方法。製造原価（製造した製品にかかった費用）→棚卸資産（在庫）→売上原価（売れた分だけの製造原価）。在庫分のコストが貸借対照表に資産として保留されるため、不良在庫を抱えていても利益があることになり得る。

■**全部原価計算**
　　売上高 net sales　　　　　　　┌製造原価 cost of manufacturing
　－売上原価 cost of sales　　←棚卸資産 inventories
　　売上総利益 net income

Index（英語）

本書で取り上げた Keywords と、Words & Phrases からの抜粋の一覧です。数字は、その語句が登場したスキットの「日付」を表します。

A

account for ~	32
accounting	36
accounts payable	18
accounts receivable	18
accumulated	9/14
achieve	13
acquisition	20
acquisition of tangible fixed assets	19
added value	14/15
adjust	22
advertising	11
affiliated company	7
agent business	29
allocate	39
annual	1
annual sales	1
assets turnover ratio	9
avoid	24/38

B

balance	39
balance sheet	1
bankrupt	1
bankruptcy with a profit	13
barrier	27
barrier to entering	28
basic fee	32
bill	15
bond issues	23
book value	12
books	18
break-even	30
break-even point (of sales)	27/30
budget	23
business practice	6
buy-out	5
buy-out fund	5

C

calculate	3/17/34
capital	2
capital investment	26/34
capital issuance	20
capital-investment-type industry	26/29
cash flow	13
cash flow from financing activities	19
cash flow from investing activities	19/24
cash flow from operating activities	18
cash flow statement	2
cash-in and cash-out	17
claim	36
class	29
committed costs	35
competition	27/31
competitor	28
connect	9
consolidated balance sheets	3
consolidated financial statements	7
consolidation	7
construction	17
consultant	29
consumer	28
contract	7
contribution profit	38
corporate bond	6/20
cost of production	10
cost of sales	10
cost of sales ratio	10
credit	15
creditor	37
current assets	1
current liabilities	1
current ratio	1
customer	28
customs duties	36
cutthroat	34

D

dead stock	10
debt relief	7
deception	36
deduct	37
defect	37
deficit-financing bond	14
define	7
depreciation	18/27/35
determine	7
development of human resources	24
devious	36
differentiate	28
direct costing	37/38
disappear	35
disclose	37
discounted cash flow (DCF)	22
distinguish	7
distribution industries	26/27
divide	34
dividend	12/20
division	3
domestic	36
dumping	36

E

earn	17

economy of scale	29	
efficiently	9	
enormous	15/27	
equal to	27	
equipment	19	
equity method	7	
equity ratio	2/5	
EU's index	14	
exceed	3/15/19/27	
exception	29	
exchangeable	30	
expenditure	20/23	
expense	10/17/24	
expenses without cash expenditures	18	
extraordinary	12	

F

fallacy of composition	34
figure	1
financial accounting	37
financial improvement	21
financial leverage	6
financial performance	21
financial statements	2
financing	2
fiscal deficit	9/13/15
fiscal year	9
fixed assets	2
fixed costs	26/27
fluctuate	18
fluctuation	12
forecast	13/22
free cash flow	21
free of charge	32
fuel charge	30
full costing	37/38
fundamental fiscal balance	13
future cash flow	22
future investments	19

G

general account budget 23

generate	27
globally	4
go broke	9
go through	38
goods	9
government bond repayment	13
gross domestic product (GDP)	14
gross profit	10

H

handling	36
hidden assets	5
hike	29
household accounts	12
hybrid car	19

I

import duty	36
improve	9
improvement	23
income statement	2/36
incur	12
index	4/9
inequality	35
insolvency	7
interest-bearing	7
invent	31
inventory	10/37
invest	3
investment	28
involve	38
issue	3
IT company	26
IT industry	26

J

joint procurement 7

L

LCD (Liquid Crystal Display)	34
leased assets	20
legal	37

lever	6
liabilities	1/4
liabilities with interest	3/4/6/22
limit	27
Linear Express	17
liquidate	2
loan	6
local allocation tax grants	23

M

machinery	19
make a loss	21
make up for	19
managerial	14
managerial accounting	37
manufacturer	34
manufacturing	2
manufacturing cost	36
marginal profit	30/32/38
maturity date	15
method	31
monopoly	31

N

national debt service	23
negative	17/20
net assets	2/4
net income	4/5/37
net profit	11
net sales	9
non-operating profit and loss	12

O

obtain	9/22
offset	36
operate	28/35
operating profit	11
operating profit ratio	28
operation	2
ordinary profit	11
outflow	23
over-production	34

over-supply 34
own 26

P

performance 20
personnel expense 11/31/36
plant and equipment 21
positive 20
president 14
primary balance 13
principle 23
procurement 19
product 10
production 11
profitable 26/38
profit-making mechanism 26
prosper 24
prosperity 23
public works 17
publicity 28
purchase 3/20/30/35
purchasing 11

Q

quantity 34

R

rational 34
reciprocal 6
recover 34
refinance 15
refinancing bond 15
registration 32
regular price 30
reorganization 20
repay 14
repayments 20
return 3
return on assets (ROA) 4/6
return on equity (ROE) 5/6

returns to the shareholders 21
revenue 23
risk premium 3

S

sales strategy 7
sales value 27
save 17
securities 1/17
selling and (general) administrative expenses ratio 11
selling and general administrative expenses 11
service 13
service life 35
settlement 7
shareholder 3
short-term liquidity 1
shrink 9
social security 23
special gains 12
special losses 12
stability 1/6
staff 24
steel manufacturer 27
stock 10/37/38
stock price 4
strategic 3
subcontractor 7
subsidiary 7
subtract 18
subtraction 22
successful 29
successful company 24
sue 36
summarize 27
supply and demand 39
sure profit 26
synonymous with 32

T

takeover bid 5

tangible fixed assets 19
tax accounting 37
tax and stamp revenues 23
tax effect accounting 12
tax revenues 13
telecommunication fees 32
terrestrial digital television broadcasting 34
three financial statements 9/17
tight 15
time 22
trading company 29
transportation expense 36
trillion 4/9/15

U

undercapitalized 2
unreasonably low prices 36
utilities 11

V

valuation loss 17
variable 27
variable costs 26/27/31
variable ratio 27
vary 36
vast 7
vice versa 17
viewpoint 30
virtual shopping mall 28
virtual space 28
V-shaped recovery 19

W

weighted average of cost of capital (WACC) 4
wholesale 26
work out 38

Index（日本語）

本書で取り上げた財務に関する用語の一覧です。解説や英語訳を探すのにお役立てください。数字は、その語句が登場したスキットの「日付」を表します。

英字

TOB（株式の公開買い付け）	5
V字回復	19

あ行

赤字国債	14
安定性、持続性	1/6
一般会計予算	23
訴える	36
売上原価	10
売上原価率	10
売上総利益	10
売上高	9
売上高営業利益率	28
売掛金	18
運転する、経営する	28/35
営業外損益	12
営業キャッシュフロー	18
営業利益	11
液晶ディスプレー	34
卸売り	26

か行

買掛金	18
会計（処理）	36
開示する、公開する	37
家計簿	12
加重平均資本調達コスト（WACC）	4
稼ぐ、得る	17
仮想商店街	28
株価	4
株主	3
株主還元	21
借換え債	15
借り換える、資金を補充する	15
関税	36
管理会計	37
関連会社	7
機械（類）	19
基礎的財政収支	13
規模のメリット	29
基本料金	32
逆数	6
キャッシュフロー	13
キャッシュフロー計算書	2
供給過剰	34
競争	27/31
競争相手、競合他社	28
共同購買	7
黒字倒産	13
経常利益	11
契約する	7
欠陥、不備、短所	37
限界利益	38
減価償却（費）	18/27/35
現金の出入り（収支）	17
建設、建造、建築	17
原理、原則、正道	23
交換可能な	30
公共工事	17
公共料金	11
貢献利益	38
公債の発行	23
控除する、差し引く	37
合成の誤謬（ごびゅう）	34
購入（する）、購買、仕入れ	3/11/20/30/35
子会社	7
顧客	28
国債の元金払い	13
国債費	23
国内総生産（GDP）	14
国内向けの、自国の	36
固定資産	2
固定費	26/27
コミティッドコスト	35
コンサルティング会社	29

さ行

債権者	37
在庫	10/37/38
歳出	23
歳出、支出	23
財政赤字	9/13/15
歳入（国家の）	23
再編成、改造、革新	20
債務免除	7
財務会計	37
財務改善	21
財務キャッシュフロー	19
財務三表	9/17
財務実績	21
財務諸表	2
財務レバレッジ	6
差し引く、控除する	18
参入障壁	28
事業、運営	2
資金調達	2
資金不足の	2
自己資本比率	2/5
資産回転率	9
資産利益率（ROA）	4/6
指数、指標	4/9
下請け企業	7
支払額、費用	20
支払い不能、破産状態	7
自己資本利益率（ROE）	5/6
資本	2
資本投資、設備投資	26
社会保障	23
社債	6/20
社長、代表取締役	14
収益構造	26
取得、獲得	20
手法、方式	31
需要と供給	39
純資産	2/4
純利益	4/5
障害物、障壁	27
償還期日	15
商社	29
消費者	28
商品、物品	9
将来のキャッシュフロー	22
人件費	11/31/36
人材育成	24
信用（度）	15
数量、価格	1
成果、パフォーマンス	20
請求書、ツケ	15
税効果会計	12
清算、決済	7
生産過剰	34
清算する、（会社を）解体する	2
生産設備	21
税収、歳入	13
製造	11
製造業者、メーカー	34
製造原価	10
製造コスト	36
製品、生産物	10
税務会計	37
設備、装置	19
設備投資	28/34
設備投資型産業	26/29
全部原価計算	37/38
増資	20
租税及び印紙収入	23
損益計算書	2/36
損益分岐点	30
損益分岐点（売上高）	27
損失を出す	21

た行

貸借対照表	1
耐用年数	35
代理業務、仲介業	29
確かな収益	26
棚卸資産	10/37
騙し、いかさま	36
ダンピング、不当に価格を下げること	36
地上波デジタルテレビ放送	34
地方交付税交付金	23
知名度	28
兆	4/9/15
調達、入手	19
帳簿、会計簿	18
帳簿価額	12
直接原価計算	37/38
通話料	32

定価、正規の値段	30
ディスカウンティッド・キャッシュフロー	22
てこ、てこ棒	6
鉄鋼メーカー	27
手元流動性	1
当期純利益	11/37
投資キャッシュフロー	19/24
投資する	3
登録	32
独占状態	31
特別損失	12
特別利益	12

な行

値上げ	29
年間売上高	1
年次の、1年の	1
年度	9
燃料費	30

は行

売却価格	27
買収	5
配当（金）	12/20
ハイブリッド車	19
ハゲタカファンド	5
破産する	1
繁栄、成功	23
繁栄する、繁盛する	24
販管費率	11
販売戦略	7
販売費及び一般管理費、販管費	11
ビジネス手法	6
費用、経費、支出	10/17/24
評価損	17
付加価値	14/15
含み益	5
不公平、不平等	35
負債	1/4
不正な、ごまかした	36
不当廉価	36
部門	3
プライマリーバランス	13
フリーキャッシュフロー	21
不良在庫	10
返済、払い戻し	20

返済する、（お金を）払い戻す	14
変動、ばらつき	12
変動する（形）	27
変動する（動）、上下する	18
変動比率	27
変動費	26/27/31
法律上の	37

ま行

マイナスの数字	17/20
増し分	30/32
見方、観点	30
未来投資	19
無料で	32
持分法	7

や行

有価証券、債券	1/17
有形固定資産	19
有形固定資産の取得	19
融資	6
有利子負債	3/4/6/22
優良企業	24
輸送費	36
輸入税	36
良くなること、改善	23
予算	23
予測（する）、見通し	13/22

ら行

リース資産	20
リスクプレミアム	3
利付き	7
利回り	3
流通業	26/27
流動資産	1
流動比率	1
流動負債	1
累積した	9/14
例外、特例	29
連結、整理統合	7
連結財務諸表	7
連結貸借対照表	3

グローバル社会で活躍するニッポン人を目指して

経済たまごシリーズ① 経済英語 はじめて学ぶ

経済英語を「はじめて学ぶ」入門書

英語を通して、経済活動を理解する基礎力を養成する、4冊組みの自習用教材。「基礎編」と「金融・国際経済編」からなるワークブック2冊（CD各1枚付き）と、経済の基本的なしくみを日本語で解説したレファレンスブック、およびインタビューブックで構成された、グローバル社会での活躍を目指す若手社会人や大学生におすすめの教材です。大学入試レベルの英語力から始められます。

Kit1・2 ワークブック【基礎編】＋ワークブック【金融・国際経済編】

経済英語の基礎力を養います。『The Nikkei Weekly』などに掲載された記事を、CDを聞きながら読んでいきます。

■日々の学習

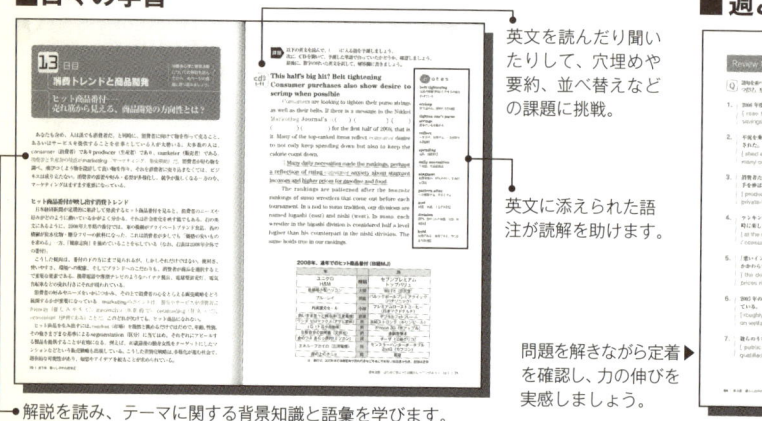

■週ごとのおさらい

英文を読んだり聞いたりして、穴埋めや要約、並べ替えなどの課題に挑戦。

英文に添えられた語注が読解を助けます。

問題を解きながら定着を確認し、力の伸びを実感しましょう。

解説を読み、テーマに関する背景知識と語彙を学びます。

Kit3 レファレンスブック「これだけは押さえておきたい経済のしくみ」

ビジネスの基本を英語で学ぶことを狙いとする『The Nikkei Weekly』のコラムから厳選して日本語訳を掲載しています。

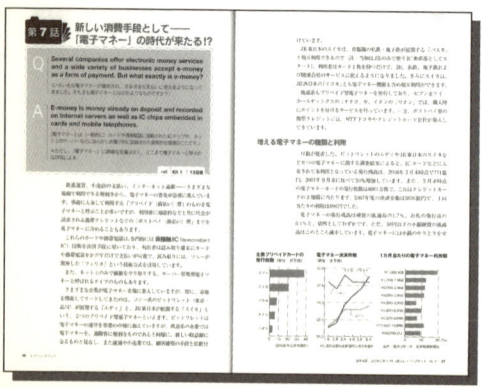

Kit4 インタビューブック

「キャリアの軌跡―走り続けるには英語が必要だ」

元P&Gヴァイスプレジデントと早稲田大学国際教養学部長にジャーナリストの蟹瀬誠一氏が尋ねます。ノーベル賞経済学者ジョセフ・E・スティグリッツ氏のインタビューにも注目です。

▲Q&Aは、英語と日本語の対訳になっています。質問の仕方や答え方のお手本として読み比べてみましょう。

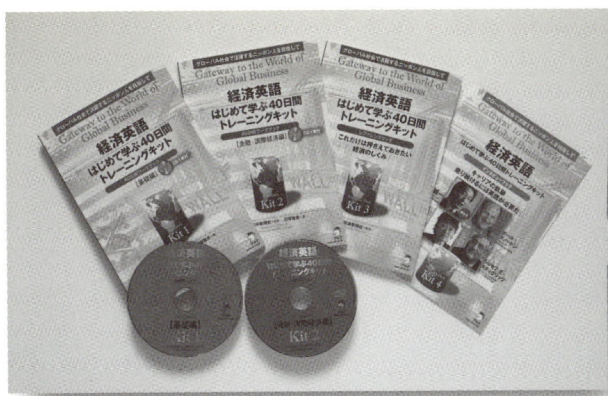

40日間トレーニングキット

アルク
www.alc.co.jp

経済英語 はじめて学ぶ40日間トレーニングキット

日本経済新聞社 監修／石塚雅彦 著　価格5,775円（税込）

商品構成
本（A5判、4冊組み・箱入　Kit 1：128ページ、
Kit 2：128ページ、Kit 3：112ページ、Kit 4：32ページ）
＋CD2枚（Kit 1約57分、Kit 2約72分）　※CDには、Kit1、2のニュース英文と単語を復習するための
　　　　　　　　　　　　　　　　　　　　チャンツ、および英語対談が収録されています。

お支払い方法
クレジットカード（一括）、
代金引換（一括、代引手数料315円）、郵便局・コンビニ払込（一括、手数料無料）

> 「経済英語を学ぶことは、内外の人々とつながるための共通のツールを手に入れることです」
> 柿木英人（日本経済新聞社、『The Nikkei Weekly』編集長）
> ──Kit 1 ワークブック【基礎編】はしがきより

お申し込みは、下記の方法で！

アルク・オンラインショップ
商品の詳細がご覧になれ、お申し込みも簡単です
http://shop.alc.co.jp/

アルク・お申し込み専用フリーダイヤル
☎ 0120-120-800　（24時間受付）
※携帯電話、PHSからもご利用いただけます。

※お知らせいただいた個人情報は、資料および教材の発送、小社からの商品情報をお送りするために利用し、その目的以外での使用はいたしません。
また、お客様の個人情報に変更の必要がある場合は、カスタマーサービス部（TEL.03-3327-1101）までご連絡をお願い申しあげます。

〒168-8611 東京都杉並区永福2-54-12　株式会社 アルク

原著者紹介：小宮一慶 Komiya Kazuyoshi
経営コンサルタント、株式会社小宮コンサルタンツ代表取締役。1957年大阪府生まれ、京都大学法学部卒。米国ダートマス大学エイモスタック経営大学院でMBA取得。東京銀行（現三菱東京UFJ銀行）、岡本アソシエイツ、日本福祉サービス（現セントケア・ホールディング）を経て現職。『ビジネスマンのための「発見力」養成講座』（ディスカヴァー・トゥエンティワン）、『あたりまえのことをバカになってちゃんとやる』（サンマーク出版）、『日経新聞の数字がわかる本』『日経新聞の「本当の読み方」がわかる本』（日経BP社）など著書多数。
ブログ http://komcon.cocolog-nifty.com/

経済たまごシリーズ2【会計】
英語で分かる　はじめての財務諸表　40日間トレーニング

2009年11月13日　　初刷発行
2011年2月25日　　第3刷発行

原　　　著：「1秒！」で財務諸表を読む方法（小宮一慶著／東洋経済新報社刊）
編集・制作：株式会社アルク　企画開発部
構成協力：西村 眞／佐藤倫正／名古屋大学経済学部西村ゼミ（清水美穂／伊藤康明／國枝由佳／村田有機／櫻井郁香／坂井直樹／山田伊織／李 墨杰／山内祥世）
英訳協力：(株)SIA（佐々木インターナショナルアカデミー）翻訳部／渡辺芳也
編集協力：小林 敬／西岡敏郎／棟石理実
英文校正：Peter Branscombe ／ Owen Schaefer

装丁：花村 広（花村デザイン事務所）
本文デザイン・DTP：有限会社ギルド

ナレーション：Deirdre Merrell-Ikeda ／ Jeff Manning
収録：音工房タック／有限会社ログスタジオ
CD制作：株式会社アドエイ
CDプレス：株式会社学習研究社
印刷・製本：広研印刷株式会社

発行人：平本照麿
発行所：株式会社アルク
〒168-8611 東京都杉並区永福2-54-12
TEL 03-3327-1101（カスタマーサービス部）
編集部 e-mail アドレス：ceee@alc.co.jp

本に落丁や乱丁、CDに不具合があった場合は、お取り替えいたします。弊社カスタマーサービス部（電話：03-3327-1101　受付時間：平日9時～17時）までご相談ください。
定価はカバーに表示してあります。

© 2009 by ALC Press Inc. Printed in Japan
PC: 7009168

地球人ネットワークを創る
アルクのシンボル「地球人マーク」です。